THE NURSERY RHYMES
OF ENGLAND

THE NURSERY RHYMES OF ENGLAND

Collected chiefly from Oral Tradition by

JAMES ORCHARD
HALLIWELL

Decorations by
MAUREEN ROFFEY

THE BODLEY HEAD
LONDON SYDNEY
TORONTO

The Nursery Rhymes of England was first published in 1842 in an edition produced for the Percy Society (see Publisher's Note on p. vi)

ISBN 0 370 01254 2
Illustrations © The Bodley Head Ltd 1970
Printed and bound in Great Britain for
The Bodley Head Ltd
9 Bow Street, London WC2
by W. & J. Mackay & Co. Ltd, Chatham
Set in 'Monotype' Ehrhardt
This edition first published 1970

Contents

PUBLISHER'S NOTE

The Nursery Rhymes of England was first published in 1842 in a private edition for the Percy Society, of which James Orchard Halliwell was a founder member. There was a second edition bearing the imprint of John Russell Smith, Soho Square, in 1843, "with alterations and additions", a third in 1844, and a fourth in 1846, with illustrations, with additions and with the contents rearranged. The British Museum Catalogue records two further editions in 1853 and *c.* 1860 and then the linking of *The Nursery Rhymes* with Halliwell's other collection, *Popular Rhymes and Nursery Tales*, in one large volume published by Warne *c.* 1870. It is from here that copy for this present edition has been taken, and our thanks go to the City of Nottingham Public Libraries for allowing us to borrow their precious copy from which to work.

The Nursery Rhymes of England served as the basis for nursery rhyme collections for over a century, being the first and probably the only attempt to be comprehensive until the Opies' publication in 1951. Joseph Jacobs owes much to Halliwell as can be seen in the notes to his fairy tale collections; Beatrix Potter records in the original version of *The Tailor of Gloucester*, "Most of the rhymes are from J. O. Halliwell's collection". Many people working in the field today have heard of Halliwell, few have seen his books.

As a young man James Orchard Halliwell was something of a prodigy, publishing his first book, a life of Sir Samuel Morland, in 1839 when he was only eighteen. In that same year he attempted to sell to the book collector Sir Thomas Phillipps some manuscripts that were later believed to have been stolen from the library of Trinity College, Cambridge, where Halliwell had matriculated in 1837, and which were subsequently sold to the British Museum. In 1845 the matter was made public and although Halliwell was by now a noted Shakespearean scholar he was barred from the British Museum and his reader's ticket withdrawn. However the lawyers of the Museum and of Trinity College "fell out" over the prosecution and the case was abandoned in 1846, Halliwell once again being given access to the Museum. In 1842 he had eloped with Phillipps' daughter, Henrietta, and on the death of her father in 1872 was forced to change his name to Halliwell-Phillipps in order to be eligible to inherit the old man's considerable fortune.

Preface to
the Fifth Edition

The great encouragement which has been given by the public to the previous editions of this little work, satisfactorily proves that, notwithstanding the extension of serious education to all but the very earliest periods of life, there still exists an undying love for the popular remnants of the ancient Scandinavian nursery literature. The infants and children of the nineteenth century have not, then, deserted the rhymes chanted so many ages since by the mothers of the North. This is a "great nursery fact"—a proof that there is contained in some of these traditional rhymes a meaning and a romance, possibly intelligible only to very young minds, that exercise an influence on the fancy of children. It is obvious there must exist something of this kind; for no modern compositions are found to supply altogether the place of the ancient doggrel.

The nursery rhyme is the novel and light reading of the infant scholar. It occupies, with respect to the A B C, the position of a romance which relieves the mind from the cares of a riper age. The absurdity and frivolity of a rhyme may naturally be its chief attractions to the very young; and there will be something lost from the imagination of that child, whose parents insist so much on matters of fact, that the "cow" must be made, in compliance with the rules of their educational code, to jump *"under"* instead of *"over* the moon"; while of course the little dog must be considered as "barking", not "laughing" at the circumstance.

These, or any such objections,—for it seems there are others of about equal weight,—are, it appears to me, more silly than the worst nursery rhyme the little readers will meet with in the following pages. I am quite willing to leave the question to their decision, feeling assured the catering for them has not been in vain, and that these cullings from the high-ways and bye-ways—they have been collected from nearly every county in England—will be to them real flowers, soothing the misery of many an hour of infantine adversity.

1853   JAMES ORCHARD HALLIWELL

Historical

I

Old King Cole
Was a merry old soul,
And a merry old soul was he;
He called for his pipe,
And he called for his bowl,
And he called for his fiddlers three.
Every fiddler, he had a fiddle,
And a very fine fiddle had he;
Twee tweedle dee, tweedle dee, went the fiddlers.
Oh, there's none so rare,
As can compare
With King Cole and his fiddlers three!

The traditional Nursery Rhymes of England commence with a
legendary satire on King Cole, who reigned in Britain, as the old
chroniclers inform us, in the third century after Christ. According to Robert of Gloucester, he was the father of St Helena, and
if so, Butler must be wrong in ascribing an obscure origin to the
celebrated mother of Constantine. King Cole was a brave and
popular man in his day, and ascended the throne of Britain on

I

the death of Asclepiod, amidst the acclamations of the people, or, as Robert of Gloucester expresses himself, the "folc was tho of this lond y-paid wel y-nou". At Colchester there is a large earthwork, supposed to have been a Roman amphitheatre, which goes popularly by the name of "King Cole's kitchen". According to Jeffrey of Monmouth, King Cole's daughter was well skilled in music, but we unfortunately have no evidence to show that her father was attached to that science, further than what is contained in the foregoing lines, which are of doubtful antiquity. The following version of the song is of the seventeenth century, the one given above being probably a modernization:

> Good King Cole,
> He call'd for his bowl,
> And he call'd for fiddlers three:
> And there was fiddle fiddle,
> And twice fiddle fiddle,
> For 'twas my lady's birth-day;
> Therefore we keep holiday,
> And come to be merry.

2

> When good king Arthur ruled this land,
>   He was a goodly king;
> He stole three pecks of barley-meal,
>   To make a bag-pudding.
>
> A bag-pudding the king did make,
>   And stuff'd it well with plums;
> And in it put great lumps of fat,
>   As big as my two thumbs.
>
> The king and queen did eat thereof,
>   And noblemen beside;
> And what they could not eat that night,
>   The queen next morning fried.

3

The following song relating to Robin Hood, the celebrated out-law, is well known at Worksop, in Nottinghamshire, where it constitutes one of the nursery series.

Robin Hood, Robin Hood,
Is in the mickle wood!
Little John, Little John,
He to the town is gone.

Robin Hood, Robin Hood,
Is telling his beads,
All in the green wood,
Among the green weeds.

Little John, Little John,
If he comes no more,
Robin Hood, Robin Hood,
He will fret full sore!

4

The following lines were obtained in Oxfordshire. The story to which it alludes is related by Matthew Paris.

One moonshiny night
As I sat high,
Waiting for one
To come by;
The boughs did bend,
My heart did ache
To see what hole the fox did make.

5

The following perhaps refers to Joanna of Castile, who visited the court of Henry VII in the year 1506.

I had a little nut-tree, nothing would it bear
But a silver nutmeg and a golden pear;
The king of Spain's daughter came to visit me,
And all was because of my little nut-tree.
I skipp'd over water, I danced over sea,
And all the birds in the air couldn't catch me.

6

From a MS. in the old Royal Library, in the British Museum, the exact reference to which is mislaid. It is written, if I recollect rightly, in a hand of the time of Henry VIII in an older manuscript.

> We make no spare
> Of John Hunkes' mare;
> And now I
> Think she will die;
> He thought it good
> To put her in the wood,
> To seek where she might ly dry;
> If the mare should chance to fale,
> Then the crownes would for her sale.

7

From MS. Sloane, 1489, fol. 19, written in the time of Charles I.

> The king of France, and four thousand men,
> They drew their swords, and put them up again.

8

In a tract, called "Pigges Corantoe, or Newes from the North", 4to. Lond. 1642, p. 3, this is called "Old Tarlton's Song". It is perhaps a parody on the popular epigram of "Jack and Jill". I do not know the period of the battle to which it appears to allude, but Tarlton died in the year 1588, so that the rhyme must be earlier.

> The king of France went up the hill,
>   With forty thousand men;
> The king of France came down the hill,
> And ne'er went up again.

Profound peace had continued for twenty-years together, when Henry IV fell upon some great martial design, the bottom whereof is not known to this day; and being rich (for he had heaped up in the Bastile a mount of gold that was as high as a lance) he levied a huge army of 40,000 men, whence came the song, *The King of France with forty thousand men*, and upon a sudden he put this army in perfect equipage, and some say he invited our Prince Henry to come unto him to be a sharer in his exploits. But going one afternoon to the Bastile, to see his treasure and ammunition, his coach stopped suddenly, by reason of some colliers and other carts that were in that narrow street; whereupon, one Ravaillac, a lay Jesuit (who had a whole twelvemonth watched an opportunity to do the act), put his foot boldly upon one of the wheels of the coach, and with a long knife stretched himself over their shoulders who were in the boot of the coach, and reached the king at the end, and stabbed him right in the left side to the heart.

9

The king of France with twenty thousand men,
Went up the hill, and then came down again;
The king of Spain, with twenty thousand more,
Climb'd the same hill the French had climb'd before.

10

Another version. The nurse sings the first line, and repeats it, time after time, until the expectant little one asks, What next? Then comes the climax.

The king of France, the king of France, with forty thousand men,
Oh, they all went up the hill, and so—came back again!

11

At the siege of Belle-isle
I was there all the while,
All the while, all the while,
At the siege of Belle-isle.

12

The tune to the following may be found in the "English Dancing Master", 1651, p. 37.

The rose is red, the grass is green,
Serve Queen Bess our noble queen;
Kitty the spinner
Will sit down to dinner,

And eat the leg of a frog;
All good people
Look over the steeple,
And see the cat play with the dog.

13

Good Queen Bess was a glorious dame,
When bonny King Jemmy from Scotland came;
We'll pepper their bodies,
Their peaceable noddies,
And give them a crack of the crown!

14

The word *tory* has changed greatly in its meaning, it originated
in the reign of Elizabeth, and represented a class of "bog-trot-
ters", who were a compound of the knave and the highwayman.
For many interesting particulars see Crofton Croker's "Re-
searches in the South of Ireland", 4to. 1824, p. 52.

Ho! Master Teague, what is your story?
I went to the wood and kill'd a *tory*;
I went to the wood and kill'd another;
Was it the same, or was it his brother?

I hunted him in, and I hunted him out,
Three times through the bog, about and about;
When out of a bush I saw his head,
So I fired my gun, and I shot him dead.

15

Please to remember
The fifth of November,
   Gunpowder treason and plot;
I know no reason
Why gunpowder treason
   Should ever be forgot.

16

Taken from MS. Douce, 357, fol. 124. See Echard's "History of England", book iii. chap. 1.

> See saw, sack-a-day;*
> Monmouth is a pretie boy,
>   Richmond is another,
> Grafton is my onely joy,
> And why should I these three destroy,
>   To please a pious brother!

* Antipodes. *c*. BROME. 1640 41. J. Okes, *for* Francis Constable.

> *Let.* Trouble not your head with my conceite,
> But minde your part. Let me not see you act now,
> In your Scholasticke way, you brought to towne wi' you
> With see saw sacke a downe, like a Sawyer.

17

> Over the water, and over the lea,
> And over the water to Charley.
> Charley loves good ale and wine,
> And Charley loves good brandy,
> And Charley loves a pretty girl,
> As sweet as sugar-candy.
>
> Over the water, and over the sea,
> And over the water to Charley.
> I'll have none of your nasty beef,
> Nor I'll have none of your barley;
> But I'll have some of your very best flour;
> To make a white cake for my Charley.

18

The following is partly quoted in an old song in a MS. at Oxford, Ashmole, No. 36, fol. 113.

> As I was going by Charing Cross
> I saw a black man upon a black horse;

They told me it was King Charles the First;
Oh dear! my heart was ready to burst!

19

High diddle ding,
Did you hear the bells ring?
The parliament soldiers are gone to the king!
Some they did laugh, some they did cry,
To see the parliament soldiers pass by.

20

High ding a ding, and ho ding a ding,
The parliament soldiers are gone to the king;
Some with new beavers, some with new bands,
The parliament soldiers are all to be hang'd.

21

Hector Protector was dressed all in green;
Hector Protector was sent to the Queen.
The Queen did not like him,
Nor more did the King:
So Hector Protector was sent back again.

22

The following is a fragment of a song on the subject, which was
introduced by Russell in the character of Jerry Sneak.

Poor old Robinson Crusoe!
Poor old Robinson Crusoe!
They made him a coat
Of an old nanny goat,
   I wonder how they could do so!
With a ring a ting tang,
With a ring a ting tang,
   Poor old Robinson Crusoe!

23

Written on occasion of the marriage of Mary, the daughter of James duke of York, afterwards James II, with the young Prince of Orange. The song from which these lines are taken may be seen in "The Jacobite Minstrelsy", 12mo, Glasgow, 1828, p. 28.

What is the rhyme for *poringer*?
The king he had a daughter fair,
And gave the Prince of Orange her.

24

The following nursery song alludes to William III and George prince of Denmark.

William and Mary, George and Anne,
Four such children had never a man:
They put their father to flight and shame,
And call'd their brother a shocking bad name.

25

A song on King William III.

As I walk'd by myself,
And talk'd to myself,
    Myself said unto me,
Look to thyself,
Take care of thyself,
    For nobody cares for thee.

I answer'd myself,
And said to myself
    In the self-same repartee,
Look to thyself,
Or not look to thyself,
    The self-same thing will be.

26

From MS. Sloane, 1489, fol. 19, written in the time of Charles
I. It appears from MS. Harl. 390, fol. 85, that these verses were
written in 1626, against the Duke of Buckingham.

There was a monkey climb'd up a tree,
When he fell down, then down fell he.

There was a crow sat on a stone,
When he was gone, then there was none.

There was an old wife did eat an apple,
When she had eat two, she had eat a couple.

There was a horse going to the mill,
When he went on, he stood not still.

There was a butcher cut his thumb,
When it did bleed, then blood did come.

There was a lackey ran a race,
When he ran fast, he ran apace.

There was a cobbler clouting shoon,
When they were mended, they were done.

There was a chandler, making candle,
When he them strip, he did them handle.

There was a navy went into Spain,
When it return'd it came again.

27

The following may possibly allude to King George and the
Pretender.

Jim and George were two great lords,
They fought all in a churn;
And when that Jim got George by the nose,
Then George began to gern.

28

Little General Monk
Sat upon a trunk,
Eating a crust of bread;
There fell a hot coal
And burnt in his clothes a hole,
Now General Monk is dead.
Keep always from the fire:
If it catch your attire,
You too, like Monk, will be dead.

29

Eighty-eight wor Kirby feight,
When nivver a man was slain;
They yatt ther meaat, an drank ther drink,
An sae com merrily heaam agayn.

SECOND CLASS

Literal

30

One, two, three,
I love coffee,
And Billy loves tea.
How good you be,
One, two, three,
I love coffee,
And Billy loves tea.

31

A, B, C, tumble down D,
The cat's in the cupboard and can't see me.

32

Finis.

F for fig, J for jig,
And N for knuckle bones,

I for John the waterman,
    And S for sack of stones.

33

1, 2, 3, 4, 5!
I caught a hare alive;
    6, 7, 8, 9, 10!
I let her go again.

34

Great A, little a,
    Bouncing B!
The cat's in the cupboard,
    And she can't see.

35

One's none;
Two's some;
Three's a many;
Four's a penny;
Five is a little hundred.

36

A, B, C, and D,
Pray, playmates, agree.
E, F, and G,
Well so it shall be.
J, K, and L,
In peace we will dwell.
M, N, and O,
To play let us go.
P, Q, R, and S,
Love may we possess.

W, X, and Y,
Will not quarrel or die.
Z, and amperse-and,
Go to school at command.

37

Hickery, dickery, 6 and 7,
Alabone Crackabone 10 and 11,
Spin span muskidan;
Twiddle 'um twaddle 'um, 21.

38

Apple-pie, pudding and pancake,
All begins with an A.

39

Miss one, two, and three could never agree,
While they gossiped round a tea-caddy.

40

One, two,
Buckle my shoe;
Three, four,
Shut the door;
Five, six,
Pick up sticks;
Seven, eight,
Lay them straight;
Nine, ten,
A good fat hen;
Eleven, twelve,
Who will delve?

Thirteen, fourteen,
Maids a courting;
Fifteen, sixteen,
Maids a kissing;
Seventeen, eighteen,
Maids a waiting;
Nineteen, twenty,
My stomach's empty.

41

Pat-a-cake, pat-a-cake, baker's man!*
So I will, master, as fast as I can:
Pat it, and prick it, and mark it with T,
Put in the oven for Tommy and me.

* *Enter* Angellica *and* Gusset *with the Child.*

Ang. Come, Nurse, where are ye? here's your little charge expects ye.

Fard. Ah Doddy besse it pitty face, Doddy besse it, Doddy besse it, was its naughty Nurse gon from it, and make it cry a Bawl for bubbies, did she so, did she so, aw 'twas a paw Nurse to leave the sweet Sylds so basely, so she was, and catchee, catchee, catchee, catchee, catchee, catchee, and catchee, catchee, catchee, catchee, catchee, catchee, tum a me, tum a me, leta me do a my Nurse [*takes it from* Angellica *and sits down to suckle it.*] Mamma, says he, I want my Bubby Mamma, says he, ah Doddy besse dat pitty face of myn Sylds, and his pitty, pitty hands, and his pitty, pitty foots, and all his pitty things, and pat-a-cake, pat-a-cake, baker's man, so I will master as I can, and prick it, and prick it, and prick it, and prick it, and prick it, and throw't into the Oven.—*D'Urfey's Campaigners,* 1608.

42

Tom Thumb's Alphabet.

A was an archer, who shot at a frog;
B was a butcher, he had a great dog;
C was a captain, all covered with lace;
D was a drunkard, and had a red face;
E was an esquire, with pride on his brow;
F was a farmer, and followed the plough;

G was a gamester, who had but ill luck;
H was a hunter, and hunted a buck;
I was an innkeeper, who lov'd to bouse;
J was a joiner, and built up a house;
K was King William, once governed this land;
L was a lady, who had a white hand;
M was a miser, and hoarded up gold;
N was a nobleman, gallant and bold;
O was an oyster girl, and went about town;
P was a parson, and wore a black gown;
Q was a queen, who wore a silk slip;
R was a robber, and wanted a whip;
S was a sailor, and spent all he got;
T was a tinker, and mended a pot;
U was an usurer, a miserable elf;
V was a vintner, who drank all himself;
W was a watchman, and guarded the door;
X was expensive, and so became poor;
Y was a youth, that did not love school;
Z was a zany, a poor harmless fool.

43

A was an apple-pie:
B bit it;
C cut it;
D dealt it;
E ate it;
F fought for it;
G got it;
H had it;
J joined it;
K kept it;
L longed for it;
M mourned for it;
N nodded at it;
O opened it;
P peeped in it;

Q quartered it;
R ran for it;
S stole it;
T took it;
V viewed it;
W wanted it;
X, Y, Z, and amperse-and,
All wish'd for a piece in hand.

44

A for the ape, that we saw at the fair;
B for a blockhead, who ne'er shall go there;
C for a collyflower, white as a curd;
D for a duck, a very good bird;
E for an egg, good in pudding or pies;
F for a farmer, rich, honest, and wise;
G for a gentleman, void of all care;
H for the hound, that ran down the hare;
I for an Indian, sooty and dark;
K for the keeper that look'd to the park;
L for a lark, that soar'd in the air;
M for the mole, that ne'er could get there;
N for Sir Nobody, ever in fault;
O for an otter, that ne'er could be caught;
P for a pudding, stuck full of plums;
Q was for quartering it, see here he comes;
R for a rook, that croak'd in the trees;
S for a sailor, that plough'd the deep seas;
T for a top, that doth prettily spin;
V for a virgin of delicate mien;
W for wealth, in gold, silver, and pence;
X for old Xenophon, noted for sense;
Y for a yew, which for ever is green;
Z for the zebra, that belongs to the queen.

Tales

45

THE STORY OF CATSKIN

There once was a gentleman grand,
  Who lived at his country seat;
He wanted an heir to his land,
  For he'd nothing but daughters yet.

His lady's again in the way,
  So she said to her husband with joy,
"I hope some or other fine day,
  To present you, my dear, with a boy."

The gentleman answered gruff,
  "If't should turn out a maid or a mouse,
For of both we have more than enough,
  She shan't stay to live in my house."

The lady, at this declaration,
  Almost fainted away with pain;

But what was her sad consternation,
    When a sweet little girl came again.

She sent her away to be nurs'd,
    Without seeing her gruff papa;
And when she was old enough,
    To a school she was packed away.

Fifteen summers are fled,
    Now she left good Mrs Jervis;
To see home she was forbid,—
    She determined to go and seek service.

Her dresses so grand and so gay,
    She carefully rolled in a knob;
Which she hid in a forest away,
    And put on a Catskin robe.

She knock'd at a castle gate,
    And pray'd for charity;
They sent her some meat on a plate,
    And kept her a scullion to be.

My lady look'd long in her face,
    And prais'd her great beauty;
I'm sorry I've no better place,
    And you must our scullion be.

So Catskin was under the cook,
    A very sad life she led,
For often a ladle she took,
    And broke poor Catskin's head.

There is now a grand ball to be,
    When ladies their beauties show:
"Mrs Cook," said Catskin, "dear me,
    How much I should like to go!"

"You go with your Catskin robe,
    You dirty, impudent slut!
Among the fine ladies and lords,
    A very fine figure you'd cut."

A basin of water she took,
    And dash'd in poor Catskin's face;
But briskly her ears she shook,
    And went to her hiding-place.

She washed every stain from her skin,
    In some crystal waterfall;
Then put on a beautiful dress,
    And hasted away to the ball.

When she entered, the ladies were mute,
    Overcome by her figure and face;
But the lord, her young master, at once
    Fell in love with her beauty and grace;

He pray'd her his partner to be,
    She said "Yes!" with a sweet smiling glance;
All night with no other lady
    But Catskin our young lord would dance.

"Pray tell me, fair maid, where you live?"
    For now was the sad parting time;
But she no other answer would give,
    Than this distich of mystical rhyme,—

𝕶ind 𝕾ir, if the truth 𝕴 must tell,
𝕬t the sign of the 𝕭asin of 𝖂ater 𝕴 dwell.

Then she flew from the ball-room, and put
    On her Catskin robe again;
And slipt in unseen by the cook,
    Who little thought where she had been.

The young lord, the very next day,
    To his mother his passion betrayed;
He declared he never would rest,
    Till he found out his beautiful maid.

There's another grand ball to be,
    Where ladies their beauties show:
"Mrs Cook," said Catskin, "dear me,
    How much I should like to go!"

"You go with your Catskin robe,
   You dirty, impudent slut!
Among the fine ladies and lords,
   A very fine figure you'd cut."

In a rage the ladle she took,
   And broke poor Catskin's head;
But off she went shaking her ears,
   And swift to her forest she fled.

She washed every blood-stain off
   In some crystal waterfall;
Put on a more beautiful dress,
   And hasted away to the ball.

My lord, at the ball-room door,
   Was waiting with pleasure and pain;
He longed to see nothing so much
   As the beautiful Catskin again.

When he asked her to dance, she again
   Said "Yes!" with her first smiling glance;
And again, all the night, my young lord
   With none but fair Catskin did dance.

"Pray tell me," said he, "where you live?"
   For now 'twas the parting-time;
But she no other answer would give,
   Than this distich of mystical rhyme,—

𝕶ind 𝕾ir, if the truth 𝕴 must tell,
𝕬t the sign of the 𝕭roken-𝕷adle 𝕴 dwell.

Then she flew from the ball, and put on
   Her Catskin robe again;
And slipt in unseen by the cook,
   Who little thought where she had been.

My lord did again, the next day,
   Declare to his mother his mind,
That he never more happy should be,
   Unless he his charmer should find.

Now another grand ball is to be,
    Where ladies their beauties show:
"Mrs Cook," said Catskin, "dear me,
    How much I should like to go!"

"You go with your Catskin robe,
    You impudent, dirty slut!
Among the fine ladies and lords,
    A very fine figure you'd cut."

In a fury she took the skimmer,
    And broke poor Catskin's head:
But heart-whole and lively as ever,
    Away to her forest she fled.

She washed the stains of blood
    In some crystal waterfall;
Then put on her most beautiful dress,
    And hasted away to the ball.

My lord, at the ball-room door,
    Was waiting with pleasure and pain;
He longed to see nothing so much
    As the beautiful Catskin again.

When he asked her to dance, she again,
    Said "Yes!" with her first smiling glance;
And all the night long my young lord
    With none but fair Catskin would dance.

"Pray tell me, fair maid, where you live?"
    For now was the parting-time;
But she no other answer would give,
    Than this distich of mystical rhyme,—

𝕶ind 𝕾ir, if the truth 𝕴 must tell,
𝕬t the sign of the 𝕭roken-𝕾kimmer 𝕴 dwell.

Then she flew from the ball, and threw on
    Her Catskin cloak again;
And slipt in unseen by the cook,
    Who little thought where she had been.

23

But not by my lord unseen,
  For this time he followed too fast;
And, hid in the forest green,
  Saw the strange things that past.

Next day he took to his bed,
  And sent for the doctor to come;
And begg'd him no other than Catskin,
  Might come into his room.

He told him how dearly he lov'd her,
  Not to have her his heart would break:
Then the doctor kindly promised
  To the proud old lady to speak.

There's a struggle of pride and love,
  For she fear'd her son would die;
But pride at the last did yield,
  And love had the mastery.

Then my lord got quickly well,
  When he was his charmer to wed;
And Catskin, before a twelve-month,
  Of a young lord was brought to bed.

To a wayfaring woman and child,
  Lady Catskin one day sent an alms;
The nurse did the errand, and carried
  The sweet little lord in her arms.

The child gave the alms to the child,
  This was seen by the old lady-mother:
"Only see," said that wicked old woman,
  "How the beggars' brats take to each other!"

This throw went to Catskin's heart,
  She flung herself down on her knees,
And pray'd her young master and lord
  To seek out her parents would please.

They set out in my lord's own coach;
  They travelled, but nought befel

Till they reached the town hard by,
  Where Catskin's father did dwell.

They put up at the head inn,
  Where Catskin was left alone;
But my lord went to try if her father
  His natural child would own.

When folks are away, in short time
  What great alterations appear:
For the cold touch of death had all chill'd
  The hearts of her sisters dear.

Her father repented too late,
  And the loss of his youngest bemoan'd;
In his old and childless state,
  He his pride and cruelty own'd.

The old gentleman sat by the fire,
  And hardly looked up at my lord;
He had no hopes of comfort
  A stranger could afford.

But my lord drew a chair close by,
  And said, in a feeling tone,
"Have you not, sir, a daughter, I pray,
  You never would see or own?"

The old man alarm'd, cried aloud,
  "A hardened sinner am I!
I would give all my worldly goods
  To see her before I die."

Then my lord brought his wife and child
  To their home and parent's face,
Who fell down and thanks returned
  To God, for His mercy and grace.

The bells, ringing up in the tower,
  Are sending a sound to the heart;
There's a charm in the old church-bells,
  Which nothing in life can impart!

25

46

The tale of Simple Simon forms one of the chap-books, but the
following verses are those generally sung in the nursery.

Simple Simon met a pieman
  Going to the fair;
Says Simple Simon to the pieman,
  "Let me taste your ware."

Says the pieman to Simple Simon,
  "Show me first your penny."
Says Simple Simon to the pieman,
  "Indeed I have not any."

Simple Simon went a fishing
  For to catch a whale;
All the water he had got
  Was in his mother's pail.

47

Punch and Judy
  Fought for a pie;
Punch gave Judy
  A sad blow on the eye.

48

There was a crooked man, and he went a crooked mile,
He found a crooked sixpence against a crooked stile:
He bought a crooked cat, which caught a crooked mouse,
And they all lived together in a little crooked house.

49

Solomon Grundy,
Born on a Monday,
Christened on Tuesday,

Married on Wednesday,
Took ill on Thursday,
Worse on Friday,
Died on Saturday,
Buried on Sunday:
This is the end
Of Solomon Grundy.

50

Robin the Bobbin, the big-bellied Ben,
He ate more meat than fourscore men;
He ate a cow, he ate a calf,
He ate a butcher and a half;
He ate a church, he ate a steeple,
He ate the priest and all the people!
  A cow and a calf,
  An ox and a half,
  A church and a steeple,
  And all the good people,
And yet he complain'd that his stomach wasn't full.

51

There was a fat man of Bombay,
Who was smoking one sunshiny day,
When a bird, called a snipe,
Flew away with his pipe,
Which vex'd the fat man of Bombay.

52

My dear, do you know,
How a long time ago,
  Two poor little children,
Whose names I don't know,
Were stolen away on a fine summer's day,
And left in a wood, as I've heard people say.

And when it was night,
So sad was their plight,
    The sun it went down,
And the moon gave no light!
They sobb'd and they sigh'd, and they bitterly cried,
And the poor little things, they lay down and died.

And when they were dead,
The Robins so red,
    Brought strawberry leaves,
And over them spread;
    And all the day long,
    They sang them this song,
"Poor babes in the wood! poor babes in the wood!
And don't you remember the babes in the wood?"

53

There was a man, and he had nought,
    And robbers came to rob him;
He crept up to the chimney pot,
    And then they thought they had him.

But he got down on t'other side,
    And then they could not find him;
He ran fourteen miles in fifteen days,
    And never look'd behind him.

54

There was a little man,
And he had a little gun,
And he went to the brook,
And he shot a little rook;
And he took it home
To his old wife Joan,
And told her to make up a fire,
While he went back,

To fetch the little drake;
But when he got there,
The drake was fled for fear,
And like an old novice,
He turn'd back again.

55

THE STORY OF THE THREE LITTLE PIGS

Once upon a time there was an old sow with three little pigs, and as she had not enough to keep them, she sent them out to seek their fortune. The first that went off met a man with a bundle of straw, and said to him, "Please, man, give me that straw to build me a house"; which the man did, and the little pig built a house with it. Presently came along a wolf, and knocked at the door, and said,—

"Little pig, little pig, let me come in."

To which the pig answered,—

"No, no, by the hair of my chiny chin chin."

The wolf then answered to that,—

"Then I'll huff, and I'll puff, and I'll blow your house in."

So he huffed, and he puffed, and he blew his house in, and eat up the little pig.

The second little pig met a man with a bundle of furze, and said, "Please, man, give me that furze to build a house"; which the man did, and the pig built his house. Then along came the wolf, and said,—

"Little pig, little pig, let me come in."

"No, no, by the hair of my chiny chin chin."

"Then I'll puff, and I'll huff, and I'll blow your house in."

So he huffed, and he puffed, and he puffed, and he huffed, and at last he blew the house down, and he ate up the little pig.

The third little pig met a man with a load of bricks, and said, "Please, man, give me those bricks to build a house with"; so the man gave him the bricks, and he built his house with them. So the wolf came, as he did to the other little pigs, and said,—

"Little pig, little pig, let me come in."

"No, no, by the hair of my chiny chin chin."

"Then I'll huff, and I'll puff, and I'll blow your house in."

Well, he huffed, and he puffed, and he huffed, and he puffed, and he puffed, and he huffed; but he could *not* get the house down. When he found that he could not, with all his huffing and puffing, blow the house down, he said, "Little pig, I know where there is a nice field of turnips." "Where?" said the little pig. "Oh, in Mr Smith's Home-field, and if you will be ready to-morrow morning I will call for you and we will go together, and get some for dinner." "Very well," said the little pig, "I will be ready. What time do you mean to go?" "Oh, at six o'clock." Well, the little pig got up at five, and got the turnips before the wolf came—(which he did about six) —and who said, "Little pig, are you ready?" The little pig said, "Ready! I have been, and come back again, and got a nice potful for dinner." The wolf felt very angry at this, but thought that he would be *up to* the little pig somehow or other, so he said, "Little pig, I know where there is a nice apple-tree." "Where?" said the pig. "Down at Merry-garden," replied the wolf, "and if you will not deceive me I will come for you, at five o'clock to-morrow, and we will go together and get some apples." Well, the little pig bustled up the next morning at four o'clock, and went off for the apples, hoping to get back before the wolf came; but he had further to go, and had to climb the tree, so that just as he was coming down from it, he saw the wolf coming, which, as you may suppose, frightened him very much. When the wolf came up he said, "Little pig, what! are you here before me? Are they nice apples?" "Yes, very," said the little pig. "I will throw you down one"; and he threw it so far, that, while the wolf was gone to pick it up, the little pig jumped down and ran home. The next day the wolf came again, and said to the little pig, "Little pig, there is a fair at Shanklin this afternoon, will you go?" "Oh yes," said the pig, "I will go; what time shall you be ready?" "At three," said the wolf. So the little pig went off before the time as usual, and got to the fair, and bought a butter-churn, which he was going home with, when he saw the wolf coming. Then he could not tell what to do. So he got into the churn to hide, and by so doing turned it round, and it rolled down the hill with the pig in it, which frightened the wolf so much, that he ran home without going to the fair. He went to the little pig's house, and told him how frightened he had been by a great round thing which came down the hill past him. Then the little pig said, "Hah, I frightened you then. I had been to the fair and bought a butter-churn, and when I saw you, I got into it, and rolled down the hill." Then the wolf was very angry indeed, and declared he *would* eat up the little pig and that he would get down the chimney after him. When the little pig saw what he was about, he hung on the pot full of water, and made up a blazing fire, and, just as the wolf was coming down, took off the cover, and in fell the wolf; so the little pig put on the cover again in an instant, boiled him up, and ate him for supper, and lived happy ever afterwards.

56

Little Tommy Tittlemouse
Lived in a little house;
He caught fishes
In other men's ditches.

57

Little King Boggen he built a fine hall,
Pie-crust and pastry-crust, that was the wall;
The windows were made of black-puddings and white,
And slated with pancakes—you ne'er saw the like.

58

The lion and the unicorn
    Were fighting for the crown;
The lion beat the unicorn
    All round about the town.
Some gave them white bread,
    And some gave them brown;
Some gave them plum-cake,
    And sent them out of town.

59

There was a jolly miller
Lived on the river Dee,

He look'd upon his pillow,
And there he saw a flea.
  Oh! Mr Flea,
You have been biting me,
And you must die:
  So he crack'd his bones
  Upon the stones,
And there he let him lie.

60

Tom, Tom, the piper's son,
Stole a pig, and away he run!
The pig was eat, and Tom was beat,
And Tom went roaring down the street.

61

In Arthur's court Tom Thumb* did live,
  A man of mickle might;
The best of all the table round,
  And eke a doughty knight.

His stature but an inch in height,
  Or quarter of a span:
Then think you not this little knight
  Was proved a valiant man?

His father was a ploughman plain,
  His mother milk'd the cow,

* "I have an old edition of this author by me, the title of which
is more sonorous and heroical than those of later date, which, for
the better information of the reader, it may not be improper to
insert in this place, 'Tom Thumb his Life and Death wherein
is declar'd his many marvellous Acts of Manhood, full of wonder and strange merriment.' Then he adds, 'Which little Knight
liv'd in King Arthur's time, in the court of Great Britain.' Indeed, there are so many spurious editions of this piece upon
one account or other, that I wou'd advise my readers to be very
cautious in their choice."—*A Comment upon the History of T. T.*,
1711. A "project for the reprinting of Tom Thumb, with mar-
ginal notes and cuts", is mentioned in the old play of *The
Projectours*, 1665, p. 41.

Yet how that they might have a son
    They knew not what to do:

Until such time this good old man
    To learnèd Merlin goes,
And there to him his deep desires
    In secret manner shows:

How in his heart he wish'd to have
    A child, in time to come,
To be his heir, though it might be
    No bigger than his thumb.

Of which old Merlin thus foretold,
    That he his wish should have,
And so this son of stature small
    The charmer to him gave.

No blood nor bones in him should be,
    In shape, and being such
That men should hear him speak, but not
    His wandering shadow touch.

But so unseen to go or come,—
    Whereas it pleas'd him still;
Begot and born in half an hour,
    To fit his father's will.

And in four minutes grew so fast
    That he became so tall
As was the ploughman's thumb in height,
    And so they did him call—

TOM THUMB, the which the fairy queen
    There gave him to his name,
Who, with her train of goblins grim,
    Unto his christening came.

Whereas she cloth'd him richly brave,
    In garments fine and fair,
Which lasted him for many years
    In seemly sort to wear.

His hat made of an oaken leaf,
    His shirt a spider's web.
Both light and soft for those his limbs
    That were so smally bred.

His hose and doublet thistledown,
    Together weaved full fine;
His stockings of an apple green,
    Made of the outward rind;

His garters were two little hairs
    Pull'd from his mother's eye;
His boots and shoes, a mouse's skin,
    Were tann'd most curiously.

Thus like a lusty gallant, he
    Adventured forth to go,
With other children in the streets,
    His pretty tricks to show.

Where he for counters, pins and points,
    And cherry-stones did play,
Till he amongst those gamesters young
    Had lost his stock away.

Yet could he soon renew the same,
    Whereas most nimbly he
Would dive into their cherry-bags,
    And their partaker be,

Unseen or felt by any one,
    Until this scholar shut
This nimble youth into a box,
    Wherein his pins he put.

Of whom to be reveng'd, he took,
    In mirth and pleasant game,
Black pots and glasses, which he hung
    Upon a bright sunbeam.

The other boys to do the like,
    In pieces broke them quite;

For which they were most soundly whipt;
  Whereat he laughed outright.

And so Tom Thumb restrainèd was,
  From these his sports and play;
And by his mother after that
  Compell'd at home to stay.

Until such time his mother went
  A-milking of her kine;
Where Tom unto a thistle fast
  She linkèd with a twine.

A thread that held him to the same,
  For fear the blustering wind
Should blow him hence—that so she might
  Her son in safety find.

But mark the hap! a cow came by,
  And up the thistle eat;
Poor Tom withal, that, as a dock,
  Was made the red cow's meat.

Who, being miss'd, his mother went
  Him calling everwhere:
Where art thou, Tom? Where art thou, Tom?
  Quoth he, Here, mother, here!

Within the red cow's stomach here,
  Your son is swallowed up:
The which into her fearful heart,
  Most careful dolours put.

Meanwhile the cow was troubled much,
  And soon releas'd Tom Thumb;
No rest she had till out her mouth,
  In bad plight he did come.

Now after this, in sowing time,
  His father would him have
Into the field to drive his plough,
  And thereupon him gave—

A whip made of a barley-straw,
　To drive the cattle on;
Where, in a furrow'd land new sown,
　Poor Tom was lost and gone.

Now by a raven of great strength
　Away he thence was borne,
And carried in the carrion's beak,
　Even like a grain of corn,

Unto a giant's castle top,
　In which he let him fall;
Where soon the giant swallowed up
　His body, clothes and all.

But soon the giant spat him out,
　Three miles into the sea;
Whereas a fish soon took him up,
　And bore him thence away.

Which lusty fish was after caught,
　And to king Arthur sent;
Where Tom was found, and made his dwarf,
　Whereas his days he spent

Long time in lively jollity,
　Belov'd of all the court;
And none like Tom was then esteem'd,
　Among the noble sort.

Amongst his deeds of courtship done,
　His highness did command,
That he should dance a galliard brave
　Upon his queen's left hand.

The which he did, and for the same
　The king his signet gave,
Which Tom about his middle wore,
　Long time a girdle brave.

How, after this, the king would not
　Abroad for pleasure go,

But still Tom Thumb must ride with him,
 Placed on his saddle-bow.

Whereon a time when, as it rain'd
 Tom Thumb most nimbly crept
In at a button-hole, where he
 Within his bosom slept.

And being near his highness' heart,
 He crav'd a wealthy boon,
A liberal gift, the which the king
 Commanded to be done.

For to relieve his father's wants,
 And mother's, being old;
Which was, so much of silver coin
 As well his arms could hold.

And so away goes lusty Tom,
 With threepence on his back,
A heavy burthen, which might make
 His wearied limbs to crack.

So travelling two days and nights,
 With labour and great pain,
He came into the house whereat
 His parents did remain;

Which was but half a mile in space
 From good king Arthur's court,
The which, in eight and forty hours,
 He went in weary sort.

But coming to his father's door,
 He there such entrance had
As made his parents both rejoice.
 And he thereat was glad.

His mother in her apron took
 Her gentle son in haste,
And by the fire-side, within
 A walnut-shell him placed;

Whereas they feasted him three days
  Upon a hazel-nut,
Whereon he rioted so long,
  He them to charges put;

And thereupon grew wond'rous sick,
  Through eating too much meat,
Which was sufficient for a month
  For this great man to eat.

But now his business call'd him forth
  King Arthur's court to see,
Whereas no longer from the same
  He could a stranger be.

But yet a few small April drops
  Which settled in the way,
His long and weary journey forth
  Did hinder and so stay.

Until his careful father took
  A birding trunk in sport,
And with one blast, blew this his son
  Into king Arthur's court.

Now he with tilts and tournaments
  Was entertained so,
That all the best of Arthur's knights
  Did him much pleasure show:

As good Sir Lancelot du Lake,
  Sir Tristam, and Sir Guy;
Yet none compared with brave Tom Thumb
  For knightly chivalry.

In honour of which noble day,
  And for his lady's sake,
A challenge in king Arthur's court
  Tom Thumb did bravely make.

'Gainst whom these noble knights did run,
  Sir Chinon and the rest,

Yet still Tom Thumb, with matchless might,
  Did bear away the best.

At last Sir Lancelot du Lake
  In manly sort came in,
And with this stout and hardy knight
  A battle did begin.

Which made the courtiers all aghast,
  For there that valiant man,
Through Lancelot's steed, before them all,
  In nimble manner ran.

Yea, horse and all, with spear and shield,
  As hardy he was seen,
But only by king Arthur's self
  And his admired queen;

Who from her finger took a ring,
  Through which Tom Thumb made way,
Not touching it, in nimble sort,
  As it was done in play.

He likewise cleft the smallest hair
  From his fair lady's head,
Not hurting her whose even hand
  Him lasting honours bred.

Such were his deeds and noble acts,
  In Arthur's court there shone,
As like in all the world beside
  Was hardly seen or known.

Now at these sports he toil'd himself,
  That he a sickness took,
Through which all manly exercise
  He carelessly forsook.

When lying on his bed sore sick,
  King Arthur's doctor came,
With cunning skill, by physic's art,
  To ease and cure the same.

His body being so slender small,
   This cunning doctor took
A fine perspective glass, with which
   He did in secret look—

Into his sickened body down,
   And therein saw that Death
Stood ready in his wasted frame,
   To cease his vital breath.

His arms and legs consum'd as small
   As was a spider's web,
Through which his dying hour grew on,
   For all his limbs grew dead.

His face no bigger than an ant's,
   Which hardly could be seen;
The loss of which renowned knight
   Much grieved the king and queen.

And so with peace and quietness
   He left this earth below;
And up into the fairy-land
   His ghost did fading go.

Whereas the fairy-queen receiv'd,
   With heavy mourning cheer,
The body of this valiant knight,
   Whom she esteem'd so dear.

For with her dancing nymphs in green,
   She fetch'd him from his bed,
With music and sweet melody,
   So soon as life was fled;

For whom king Arthur and his knights
   Full forty days did mourn;
And in rememberance of his name
   That was so strangely born—

He built a tomb of marble grey,
   And year by year did come

To celebrate ye mournful death
    And burial of Tom Thumb.

Whose fame still lives in England here,
    Amongst the country sort;
Of whom our wives and children small
    Tell tales of pleasant sport.

62

The following lines, slightly altered, occur in a little black-letter
book by W. Wagner, printed about the year 1560; entitled, "A
very mery and pythie commedie, called, the longer thou livest,
the more foole thou art". See also a whole song, ending with
these lines, in Ritson's "North Country Chorister", 8vo,
Durham, 1802, p. 1.

Bryan O'Lin, and his wife, and wife's mother,
They all went over a bridge together:
The bridge was broken, and they all fell in,
The deuce go with all! quoth Bryan O'Lin.

63

Old Mother Goose, when
She wanted to wander,
Would ride through the air
On a very fine gander.

Mother Goose had a house,
'Twas built in a wood,
Where an owl at the door
For sentinel stood.

This is her son Jack,
A plain-looking lad,
He is not very good,
Nor yet very bad.

She sent him to market;
A live goose he bought;
Here, mother, says he,
It will not go for nought.

Jack's goose and her gander
Grew very fond;
They'd both eat together,
Or swim in one pond.

Jack found one morning,
As I have been told,
His goose had laid him
An egg of pure gold.

Jack rode to his mother,
The news for to tell,
She call'd him a good boy,
And said it was well.

Jack sold his gold egg
To a rogue of a Jew,
Who cheated him out of
The half of his due.

Then Jack went a courting
A lady so gay,
As fair as the lily,
And sweet as the May.

The Jew and the Squire,
Came behind his back,
And began to belabour
The sides of poor Jack.

Then old Mother Goose
That instant came in,
And turned her son Jack
Into fam'd Harlequin.

She then with her wand
Touch'd the lady so fine,
And turn'd her at once
Into sweet Columbine.

The gold egg into the sea
Was thrown then,—

When Jack jump'd in,
And got the egg back again.

The Jew got the goose,
Which he vow'd he would kill,
Resolving at once
His pockets to fill.

Jack's mother came in,
And caught the goose soon,
And mounting its back,
Flew up to the moon.

64

I'll tell you a story
  About Jack a Nory,—
And now my story's begun:
  I'll tell you another
  About Jack and his brother,—
And now my story's done.

65

The "foles of Gotham" are mentioned as early as the fifteenth century in the "Townley Mysteries"; and, at the commencement of the sixteenth century, Dr Andrew Borde made a collection of stories about them, not, however, including the following, which rests on the authority of nursery tradition.

Three wise men of Gotham
Went to sea in a bowl:
And if the bowl had been stronger,
My song would have been longer.

66

The following two stanzas, although they belong to the same piece, are often found separated from each other.

Robin and Richard were two pretty men;
They lay in bed till the clock struck ten;

Then up starts Robin, and looks at the sky,
Oh! brother Richard, the sun's very high:
The bull's in the barn threshing the corn,
The cock's on the dunghill blowing his horn,
The cat's at the fire frying of fish,
The dog's in the pantry breading his dish.

67

My lady Wind, my lady Wind,
Went round about the house to find
   A chink to get her foot in:
She tried the keyhole in the door,
She tried the crevice in the floor,
   And drove the chimney soot in.

And then one night when it was dark,
She blew up such a tiny spark,
   That all the house was pothered:
From it she raised up such a flame,
As flamed away to Belting Lane,
   And White Cross folks were smothered.

And thus when once, my little dears,
A whisper reaches itching ears,
   The same will come, you'll find:
Take my advice, restrain the tongue,
Remember what old nurse has sung,
   Of busy lady Wind!

68

Old Abram Brown is dead and gone,
You'll never see him more;
He used to wear a long brown coat,
   That button'd down before.

69

A dog and a cock
A journey once took,
They travell'd along till 'twas late;
   The dog he made free
   In the hollow of a tree,
And the cock on the boughs of it sate.

   The cock nothing knowing,
   In the morn fell a-crowing,
Upon which comes a fox to the tree;
   Says he, I declare,
   Your voice is above
All the creatures I ever did see.

   Oh! would you come down
   I the fav'rite might own:
Said the cock, there's a porter below;
   If you will go in,
   I promise I'll come down.
So he went—and was worried for it too.

70

Little Tom Tittlemouse,
Lived in a bell-house;
The bell-house broke,
And Tom Tittlemouse woke.

71

Tommy kept a chandler's shop,
Richard went to buy a mop;
Tommy gave him such a knock,
That sent him out of his chandler's shop.

72

When I was a little girl, about seven years old,
I hadn't got a petticoat, to cover me from the cold;

So I went into Darlington, that pretty little town,
And there I bought a petticoat, a cloak, and a gown.
I went into the woods and built me a kirk,
And all the birds of the air, they helped me to work;
The hawk with his long claws pulled down the stone,
The dove, with her rough bill, brought me them home:
The parrot was the clergyman, the peacock was the clerk,
The bullfinch play'd the organ, and we made merry work.

73

Pemmy was a pretty girl,
　　But Fanny was a better;
Pemmy look'd like any churl,
　　When little Fanny let her.

Pemmy had a pretty nose,
　　But Fanny had a better;
Pemmy oft would come to blows,
　　But Fanny would not let her.

Pemmy had a pretty doll,
　　But Fanny had a better;
Pemmy chatter'd like a poll,
　　When little Fanny let her.

Pemmy had a pretty song,
　　But Fanny had a better;
Pemmy would sing all day long,
　　But Fanny would not let her.

Pemmy loved a pretty lad,
　　And Fanny loved a better;
And Pemmy wanted for to wed,
　　But Fanny would not let her.

74

A tale for the 1st of March.

Taffy was a Welshman, Taffy was a thief,
Taffy came to my house and stole a piece of beef:

I went to Taffy's house, Taffy was not at home;
Taffy came to my house and stole a marrowbone:
I went to Taffy's house, Taffy was not in;
Taffy came to my house and stole a silver pin:
I went to Taffy's house, Taffy was in bed,
I took up a poker and flung it at his head.

75

The tale of Jack Horner has long been appropriated to the
nursery. The four lines which follow are the traditional ones,
and they form part of "The pleasant History of Jack Horner,
containing his witty Tricks and pleasant Pranks, which he plaied
from his Youth to his riper Years", 12mo; a copy of which is in
the Bodleian Library, and this extended story is in substance
the same with "The Fryer and the Boy", 12mo, Lond. 1617, and
both of them are taken from the more ancient story of "Jack
and his Stepdame", which has been printed by Mr Wright.

Little Jack Horner sat in the corner,
    Eating a Christmas pie;
He put in his thumb, and he took out a plum,
    And said, What a good boy am I !

76

There was a king, and he had three daughter,
And they all lived in a basin of water;
    The basin bended,
    My story's ended.
If the basin had been stronger,
My story would have been longer.

77

The man in the moon,
Came tumbling down,
And asked his way to Norwich.
He went by the south,
And burnt his mouth
With supping cold pease-porridge.

78

Our saucy boy Dick
Had a nice little stick,
Cut from a hawthorn tree:
And with this pretty stick,
He thought he could beat
A boy much bigger than he.

But the boy turned round,
And hit him a rebound,
Which did so frighten poor Dick,
That, without more delay,
He ran quite away,
And over a hedge he jump'd quick.

79

Moss was a little man, and a little mare did buy,
For kicking and for sprawling none her could come nigh;
She could trot, she could amble, and could canter here and there,
But one night she strayed away—so Moss lost his mare.

Moss got up next morning to catch her fast asleep,
And round about the frosty fields so nimbly he did creep.
Dead in a ditch he found her, and glad to find her there,
So I'll tell you by and by, how Moss caught his mare.

Rise! stupid, rise! he thus to her did say;
Arise, you beast, you drowsy beast, get up without delay,
For I must ride you to the town, so don't lie sleeping there;
He put the halter round her neck—so Moss caught his mare.

Proverbs

80

St Swithin's day, if thou dost rain,
For forty days it will remain:
St Swithin's day, if thou be fair,
For forty days 'twill rain na mair.

81

To make your candles last for a',
   You wives and maids give ear-o!
To put 'em out's the the only way,
   Says honest John Boldero.

82

If wishes were horses,
   Beggars would ride;
If turnips were watches,
   I'd wear one by my side.

83

Hours of sleep.

> Nature requires five,
>   Custom gives seven!
> Laziness takes nine,
>   And Wickedness eleven.

84

> Three straws on a staff,
> Would make a baby cry and laugh.

85

> See a pin and pick it up,
> All the day you'll have good luck,
> See a pin and let it lay,
> Bad luck you'll have all the day!

86

> Go to bed first, a golden purse;
> Go to bed second, a golden pheasant;
> Go to bed third, a golden bird!

87

> When the wind is in the east,
> 'Tis neither good for man nor beast;
> When the wind is in the north,
> The skilful fisher goes not forth;
> When the wind is in the south,
> It blows the bait in the fishes' mouth;
> When the wind is in the west,
> Then 'tis at the very best.

88

Bounce Buckram, velvet's dear;
Christmas comes but once a year.

89

One version of the following song, which I believe to be the
genuine one, is written on the last leaf of MS. Harl. 6580,
between the lines of a fragment of an old charter, originally
used for binding the book, in a hand of the end of the seventeenth century, but unfortunately it is scarcely adapted for the
"ears polite" of modern days.

A man of words and not of deeds,
Is like a garden full of weeds;
And when the weeds begin to grow,
It's like a garden full of snow;
And when the snow begins to fall,
It's like a bird upon the wall;
And when the bird away does fly,
It's like an eagle in the sky;
And when the sky begins to roar;
It's like a lion at the door;
And when the door begins to crack,
It's like a stick across your back;
And when your back begins to smart,
It's like a penknife in your heart;
And when your heart begins to bleed,
You're dead, and dead, and dead indeed.

90

'Tis true, we often have been told
In Proverbs very wise and old,
That men of words, and not of deeds,
Are like a garden full of weeds;
And that fine compliments and speeches,
Stuff'd full of thank ye's, and beseech ye's,

Will neither purchase what we lack,
Not fill a bushel, or a sack.

91

If you sneeze on Monday, you sneeze for danger;
Sneeze on a Tuesday, kiss a stranger;
Sneeze on a Wednesday, sneeze for a letter;
Sneeze on a Thursday, something better;
Sneeze on a Friday, sneeze for sorrow;
Sneeze on a Saturday, see your sweetheart to-morrow.

92

A pullet in the pen
Is worth a hundred in the fen!

93

He that would thrive
Must rise at five;
He that hath thriven
May lie till seven;
And he that by the plough would thrive,
Himself must either hold or drive.

94

The following is quoted in Miege's "Great French Dictionary",
fol. Lond. 1687, 2d part.

A swarm of bees in May
Is worth a load of hay;
A swarm of bees in June
Is worth a silver spoon;
A swarm of bees in July
Is not worth a fly.

95

They that wash on Monday
  Have all the week to dry;
They that wash on Tuesday
  Are not so much awry;
They that wash on Wednesday
  Are not so much to blame;
They that wash on Thursday,
  Wash for shame;
They that wash on Friday,
  Wash in need;
And they that wash on Saturday,
  Oh! they're sluts indeed.

96

Needles and pins, needles and pins,
When a man marries his trouble begins.

97

In Suffolk, children are frequently reminded of the decorum
due to the Sabbath by the following lines.

Yeow mussent sing a' Sunday,
  Becaze it is a sin,
But yeow may sing a' Monday
  Till Sunday cums agin.

98

A sunshiny shower
Won't last half an hour.

99

As the days grow longer,
The storms grow stronger.

100

As the days lengthen,
So the storms strengthen.

101

He that goes to see his wheat in May,
Comes weeping away.

102

The mackerel's cry,
Is never long dry.

103

In July,
Some reap rye;
In August,
If one will not
The other must.

104

Proverbial many years ago, when the guinea in gold was of a higher value than its nominal representative in silver.

A guinea it would sink,
And a pound it would float;
Yet I'd rather have a guinea,
Than your one pound note.

105

For every evil under the sun,
There is a remedy, or there is none.
If there be one, try and find it;
If there be none, never mind it.

106

The art of good driving's a paradox quite,
    Though custom has prov'd it so long;
If you go to the left, you're sure to go right,
    If you go to the right, you go wrong.

107

    Friday night's dream
      On the Saturday told,
    Is sure to come true,
      Be it never so old.

108

When the sand doth feed the clay,
England woe and well-a-day!
But when the clay doth feed the sand,
Then it is well with Angle-land.

109

The fair maid who, the first of May,
Goes to the fields at break of day,
And washes in dew from the hawthorn tree,
Will ever after handsome be.

Scholastic

110

A diller, a dollar,
A ten o'clock scholar,
What makes you come so soon?
You used to come at ten o'clock,
But now you come at noon.

111

Tell tale, tit!
Your tongue shall be slit,
And all the dogs in the town
Shall have a little bit.

112

The joke of the following consists in saying it so quick that it
cannot be told whether it is English or gibberish. It is remark-
able that the last two lines are quoted in MS. Sloane. 4, of the
fifteenth century, as printed in the "Reliq. Antiq.", vol. i. p.
324.

In fir tar is,
In oak none is,
In mud eel is,
In clay none is.
Goat eat ivy,
Mare eat oats.

113

The dominical letters attached to the first days of the several
months are remembered by the following lines.

At Dover Dwells George Brown Esquire,
Good Christopher Finch, And David Friar.

An ancient and graver example, fulfilling the same purpose,
runs as follows.

Astra Dabit Dominus, Gratisque Beabit Egenos,
Gratia Christicolæ Feret Aurea Dona Fideli.

114

Birch and green holly, boys,
Birch and green holly:
If you get beaten, boys,
'Twill be your own folly.

115

When V and I together meet,
They make the number Six complete.
When I with V doth meet once more,
Then 'tis they Two can make but Four.
And when that V from I is gone,
Alas! poor I can make but One.

116

Multiplication is vexation,
Division is as bad;

The Rule of Three doth puzzle me,
And Practice drives me mad.

117

The following memorial lines are by no means modern. They occur, with slight variations, in an old play, called "The Re-turne from Parnassus", 4to, Lond. 1606, and another version may be seen in Winter's "Cambridge Almanac" for 1635. See the "Rara Mathematica", p. 119.

Thirty days hath September,
April, June, and November;
February has twenty-eight alone,
All the rest have thirty-one,
Excepting leap-year, that's the time
When February's days are twenty-nine.

Thus noted by the Ancients:

But thirty days November hath,
April, June, and September;
February hath but twenty-eight,
Without a leap attender.

118

My story's ended,
My spoon is bended:
If you don't like it,
Go to the next door,
And get it mended.

119

On arriving at the end of a book, boys have a practice of reciting the following absurd lines, which form the word *finis* back-wards and forwards, by the initials of the words.

Father Iohnson Nicholas Iohnson's son—
Son Iohnson Nicholas Iohnson's Father.

To get to father Johnson, therefore, was to reach the end of the book.

120

The rose is red, the grass is green;
And in this book my name is seen.

121

Cross patch,
Draw the latch,
Sit by the fire and spin;
Take a cup,
And drink it up,
Then call your neighbours in.

122

Come when you're called,
Do what you're bid,
Shut the door after you,
Never be chid.

123

Speak when you're spoken to,
Come when one call;
Shut the door after you,
And turn to the wall!

124

I love my love with an A, because he's Agreeable;
I hate him because he's Avaricious.
He took me to the sign of the Acorn,
And treated me with Apples.
His name's Andrew,
And he lives at Arlington.

125

A laconic reply to a person who indulges much in supposition.

If ifs and ands
Were pots and pans,
There would be no need for tinkers!

126

Mistress Mary, quite contrary,
How does your garden grow?
With cockle-shells and silver bells,
And muscles all a row.

127

Doctor Faustus was a good man,
He whipt his scholars now and then;
When he whipp'd them he made them dance
Out of Scotland into France,
Out of France into Spain,
And then he whipp'd them back again!

128

A Greek bill of fare.

Legomoton,
Acapon,
Alfagheuse,
Pasti venison.

129

When I was a little boy, I had but little wit,
It is some time ago, and I've no more yet;
Nor ever ever shall, until that I die,
For the longer I live, the more fool am I.

Songs

130

Oh, where are you going,
   My pretty maiden fair,
With your red rosy cheeks,
   And your coal-black hair?
I'm going a–milking,
   Kind sir, says she;
And it's dabbling in the dew
   Where you'll find me.

May I go with you,
   My pretty maiden fair, &c.
Oh, you may go with me,
   Kind sir, says she, &c.

If I should chance to kiss you,
   My pretty maiden fair, &c.
The wind may take it off again,
   Kind sir, says she, &c.

And what is your father,
   My pretty maiden fair, &c.
My father is a farmer,
   Kind sir, says she, &c.

And what is your mother,
   My pretty maiden fair, &c.
My mother is a dairy-maid,
   Kind sir, says she, &c.

131

Polly put the kettle on,
Polly put the kettle on,
Polly put the kettle on,
   And let's drink tea.

Sukey take it off again,
Sukey take it off again,
Sukey take it off again,
   They're all gone away.

132

This is the version generally given in nursery collections, but
is somewhat different in the "Pills to Purge Melancholy", 1719,
vol. iv. p. 148.

One misty moisty morning,
When cloudy was the weather,
There I met an old man
Clothed all in leather;
Clothed all in leather,
With cap under his chin,—
How do you do, and how do you do,
And how do you do again?

133

The fox and his wife they had a great strife,
They never ate mustard in all their whole life;
They ate their meat without fork or knife,
   And loved to be picking a bone, e-ho!

The fox jumped up on a moonlight night;
The stars they were shining, and all things bright;
Oh, ho! said the fox, it's a very fine night
    For me to go through the town, e-ho!

The fox when he came to yonder stile,
He lifted his lugs and he listened a while!
Oh, ho! said the fox, it's but a short mile
    From this unto yonder wee town, e-ho!

The fox when he came to the farmer's gate,
Who should he see but the farmer's drake;
I love you well for your master's sake,
    And long to be picking your bone, e-ho!

The grey goose she ran round the hay-stack,
Oh, ho! said the fox, you are very fat;
You'll grease my beard and ride on my back
    From this into yonder wee town, e-ho!

Old Gammer Hipple-hopple hopped out of bed,
She opened the casement and popped out her head;
Oh! husband, oh! husband, the grey goose is dead,
    And the fox is gone through the town, oh!

Then the old man got up in his red cap,
And swore he would catch the fox in a trap;
But the fox was too cunning, and gave him the slip,
    And ran through the town, the town, oh!

When he got to the top of the hill,
He blew his trumpet both loud and shrill,
For joy that he was safe
    Through the town, oh!

When the fox came back to his den,
He had young ones both nine and ten,
"You're welcome home, daddy, you may go again,
If you bring us such nice meat
    From the town, oh!"

134

Little Tom Dogget,
　What dost thou mean,
To kill thy poor Colly
　Now she's so lean?
Sing, oh poor Colly,
　Colly, my cow,
For Colly will give me
　No more milk now.

I had better have kept her,
　'Till fatter she had been,
For now, I confess,
　She's a little too lean.
Sing, oh poor Colly, &c.

First in comes the tanner
　With his sword by his side,
And he bids me five shillings
　For my poor cow's hide.
Sing, oh poor Colly, &c.

Then in comes the tallow-chandler,
　Whose brains were but shallow,
And he bids me two-and-sixpence
　For my cow's tallow.
Sing, oh poor Colly, &c.

Then in comes the huntsman
　So early in the morn,
He bids me a penny
　For my cow's horn.
Sing, oh poor Colly, &c.

Then in comes the tripe-woman,
　So fine and so neat,
She bids me three half-pence
　For my cow's feet.
Sing, oh poor Colly, &c.

Then in comes the butcher,
  That nimble-tongued youth,
Who said she was carrion,
  But he spoke not the truth.
Sing, oh poor Colly, &c.

The skin of my cowly
  Was softer than silk,
And three times a-day
  My poor cow would give milk.
Sing, oh poor Colly, &c.

She every year
  A fine calf did me bring,
Which fetcht me a pound,
  For it came in the spring.
Sing, oh poor Colly, &c.

But now I have kill'd her,
  I can't her recall;
I will sell my poor Colly,
  Hide, horns, and all.
Sing, oh poor Colly, &c.

The butcher shall have her,
  Though he gives but a pound,
And he knows in his heart
  That my Colly was sound.
Sing, oh poor Colly, &c.

And when he has bought her
  Let him sell all together,
The flesh for to eat,
  And the hide for leather.
Sing, oh poor Colly, &c.

A different version of the above, commencing, My Billy
Aroma, is current in the nurseries of Cornwall. One verse runs
as follows:

      In comes the horner,
        Who roguery scorns,
      And gives me three farthings
        For poor cowly's horns.

This is better than our reading, and it concludes thus:

There's an end to my cowly,
Now she's dead and gone;
For the loss of my cowly
I sob and I mourn.

135

A north-country song.

Says t'auld man tit oak tree,
Young and lusty was I when I kenn'd thee;
I was young and lusty, I was fair and clear,
Young and lusty was I mony a lang year;
But sair fail'd am I, sair fail'd now,
Sair fail'd am I sen I kenn'd thou.

136

You shall have an apple,
You shall have a plum,
You shall have a rattle-basket,
When your dad comes home.

137

Up at Piccadilly oh!
The coachman takes his stand,
And when he meets a pretty girl,
He takes her by the hand;
Whip away for ever oh!
Drive away so clever oh!
All the way to Bristol oh!
He drives her four-in-hand.

138

The first line of this nursery rhyme is quoted in Beaumont and
Fletcher's *Bonduca*, Act v. sc. 2. It is probable also that Sir
Toby alludes to this song in *Twelfth Night*, Act ii, sc. 2, when

he says, "Come on; there is sixpence for you; let's have a song."
In *Epulario, or the Italian Banquet*, 1589, is a receipt "to make
pies so that the birds may be alive in them and flie out when
it is cut up", a mere device, live birds being introduced after
the pie is made. This may be the original subject of the following song.

Sing a song of sixpence,
 A bag full of rye;
Four and twenty blackbirds
 Baked in a pie;

When the pie was opened
 The birds began to sing;
Was not that a dainty dish
 To set before the king?

The king was in his counting house
 Counting out his money;
The queen was in the parlour
 Eating bread and honey;

The maid was in the garden
 Hanging out the clothes,
There came a little blackbird,
 And snapt off her nose.

Jenny was so mad,
 She didn't know what to do;
She put her finger in her ear,
 And crackt it right in two.

139

Lend me thy mare to ride a mile?
She is lamed, leaping over a stile.
Alack! and I must keep the fair!
I'll give thee money for thy mare.
Oh, oh! say you so?
Money will make the mare to go.

140

About the bush, Willy,
   About the bee-hive,
About the bush, Willy,
   I'll meet thee alive.

Then to my ten shillings
   Add you but a groat,
I'll go to Newcastle,
   And buy a new coat.

Five and five shillings,
   Five and a crown;
Five and five shillings,
   Will buy a new gown.

Five and five shillings,
   Five and a groat;
Five and five shillings,
   Will buy a new coat.

141

A pretty little girl in a round-eared cap
I met in the streets t'other day;
   She gave me such a thump,
   That my heart it went bump;
I thought I should have fainted away!
I thought I should have fainted away!

142

My father he died, but I can't tell you how,
He left me six horses to drive in my plough:
   With my wing wang waddle oh,
   Jack sing saddle oh,
   Blowsey boys buble oh,
   Under the broom.

I sold my six horses and I bought me a cow,
I'd fain have made a fortune but did not know how:
  With my, &c.

I sold my cow, and I bought me a calf;
I'd fain have made a fortune but lost the best half:
  With my, &c.

I sold my calf, and I bought me a cat;
A pretty thing she was, in my chimney corner sat:
  With my, &c.

I sold my cat, and bought me a mouse;
He carried fire in his tail, and burnt down my house:
  With my, &c.

143

Little Bo-peep has lost her sheep,
  And can't tell where to find them;
Leave them alone, and they'll come home,
  And bring their tails behind them.

Little Bo-peep fell fast asleep,
  And dreamt she heard them bleating;
But when she awoke, she found it a joke,
  For they still were all fleeting.

Then up she took her little crook,
  Determin'd for to find them;
She found them indeed, but it made her heart bleed,
  For they'd left all their tails behind 'em.

144

Jeanie come tie my,
Jeanie come tie my,
Jeanie come tie my bonnie cravat;
I've tied it behind,
I've tied it before,
And I've tied it so often, I'll tie it no more.

145

Trip upon trenchers, and dance upon dishes,
My mother sent me for some barm, some barm;
She bid me tread lightly, and come again quickly,
For fear the young men should do me some harm.
Yet didn't you see, yet didn't you see,
What naughty tricks they put upon me:
   They broke my pitcher,
     And spilt the water,
   And huff'd my mother,
     And chid her daughter,
And kiss'd my sister instead of me.

146

From "Histrio-mastix, or, the Player Whipt", 4to. Lond. 1610.
Mr Rimbault tells me this is common in Yorkshire.

   Some up, and some down,
     There's players in the town,
You wot well who they be;
   The sun doth arise,
     To three companies,
One, two, three, four, make wee!

   Besides we that travel,
     With pumps full of gravel,
Made all of such running leather:
   That once in a week,
     New masters we seek,
And never can hold together.

147

Johnny shall have a new bonnet,
   And Johnny shall go to the fair,
And Johnny shall have a blue ribbon
   To tie up his bonny brown hair,
And why may not I love Johnny?
   And why may not Johnny love me?

And why may not I love Johnny,
   As well as another body?
And here's a leg for a stocking,
   And here is a leg for a shoe,
And he has a kiss for his daddy,
   And two for his mammy, I trow.
And why may not I love Johnny?
   And why may not Johnny love me?
And why may not I love Johnny,
   As well as another body?

148

As I was walking o'er little Moorfields,
I saw St Paul's a running on wheels,
   With a fee, fo, fum.
Then for further frolics I'll go to France,
While Jack shall sing and his wife shall dance,
   With a fee, fo, fum.

149

The north wind doth blow,
   And we shall have snow,
And what will poor Robin do then?
                  Poor thing!
   He'll sit in a barn,
   And to keep himself warm,
Will hide his head under his wing.
                  Poor thing!

150

From W. Wager's play, called "The longer thou livest, the
more foole thou art", 4to, Lond.

The white dove sat on the castle wall,
I bend my bow and shoot her I shall;
I put her in my glove both feathers and all;
I laid my bridle upon the shelf,
If you will any more, sing it yourself.

151

Elsie Marley is grown so fine,
She won't get up to serve the swine,
But lies in bed till eight or nine,
And surely she does take her time.

And do you ken Elsie Marley, honey?
The wife who sells the barley, honey;
She won't get up to serve her swine,
And do you ken Elsie Marley, honey?

Elsie Marley is said to have been a merry alewife who lived
near Chester, and the remainder of this song relating to her
will be found in the "Chester Garland", 12mo. n.d. The first
four lines have become favourites in the nursery.

152

London bridge is broken down,
    Dance o'er my lady lee;
London bridge is broken down,
    With a gay lady.

How shall we build it up again?
    Dance o'er my lady lee;
How shall we build it up again?
    With a gay lady.

Silver and gold will be stole away,
    Dance o'er my lady lee;
Silver and gold will be stole away,
    With a gay lady.

Build it up again with iron and steel,
    Dance o'er my lady lee;
Build it up with iron and steel,
    With a gay lady.

Iron and steel will bend and bow,
    Dance o'er my lady lee!
Iron and steel will bend and bow,
    With a gay lady.

Build it up with wood and clay,
    Dance o'er my lady lee;
Build it up with wood and clay,
    With a gay lady.

Wood and clay will wash away,
    Dance o'er my lady lee;
Wood and clay will wash away,
    With a gay lady.

Build it up with stone so strong,
    Dance o'er my lady lee;
Huzza! 'twill last for ages long,
    With a gay lady.

153

Old Father of the Pye,
I cannot sing, my lips are dry;
But when my lips are very well wet,
Then I can sing with the Heigh go Bet!

This appears to be an old hunting song. *Go bet* is a very ancient sporting phrase, equivalent to *go along*. It occurs in Chaucer, Leg. Dido, 288.

154

Part of this is in a song called "Jockey's Lamentation", in the "Pills to Purge Melancholy", 1719, vol. v. p. 317.

Tom he was a piper's son,
He learn'd to play when he was young,
But all the tunes that he could play,
Was, "Over the hills and far away";
Over the hills, and a great way off,
And the wind will blow my top-knot off.

Now Tom with his pipe made such a noise,
That he pleased both the girls and boys,
And they stopp'd to hear him play,
"Over the hills and far away".

Tom with his pipe did play with such skill,
That those who heard him could never keep still;
Whenever they heard they began for to dance,
Even pigs on their hind legs would after him prance.

As Dolly was milking her cow one day,
Tom took out his pipe and began for to play;
So Doll and the cow danced "the Cheshire round",
Till the pail was broke, and the milk ran on the ground.

He met old Dame Trot with a basket of eggs,
He used his pipe, and she used her legs;
She danced about till the eggs were all broke,
She began for to fret, but he laughed at the joke.

He saw a cross fellow was beating an ass,
Heavy laden with pots, pans, dishes, and glass;
He took out his pipe and played them a tune,
And the jackass's load was lightened full soon.

155

Jacky, come give me thy fiddle,
    If ever thou mean to thrive?
Nay; I'll not give my fiddle
    To any man alive.

If I should give my fiddle,
    They'll think that I'm gone mad;
For many a joyful day
    My fiddle and I have had.

156

The following lines are part of an old song, the whole of which
may be found in "Deuteromelia", 1609, and also in MS.
Additional, 5336, fol. 5.

Of all the gay birds that e'er I did see,
The owl is the fairest by far to me;
For all the day long she sits on a tree,
And when the night comes away flies she.

157

I love sixpence, pretty little sixpence,
  I love sixpence better than my life;
I spent a penny of it, I spent another,
  And took fourpence home to my wife.

Oh, my little fourpence, pretty little fourpence,
  I love fourpence better than my life;
I spent a penny of it, I spent another,
  And I took twopence home to my wife.

Oh, my little twopence, my pretty little twopence,
  I love twopence better than my life;
I spent a penny of it, I spent another,
  And I took nothing home to my wife.

Oh, my little nothing, my pretty little nothing,
  What will nothing buy for my wife?
I have nothing, I spend nothing,
  I love nothing better than my wife.

158

Merry are the bells, and merry would they ring,
Merry was myself, and merry could I sing;
With a merry ding-dong, happy, gay, and free,
And a merry sing-song, happy let us be!

Waddle goes your gait, and hollow are your hose,
Noddle goes your pate, and purple is your nose;
Merry is your sing-song, happy, gay, and free,
With a merry ding-dong, happy let us be!

Merry have we met, and merry have we been,
Merry let us part, and merry meet again;
With our merry sing-song, happy, gay, and free,
And a merry ding-dong, happy, let us be!

159

My maid Mary
She minds her dairy,
While I go a hoing and mowing each morn;
Merrily run the reel,
And the little spinning wheel,
Whilst I am singing and mowing my corn.

160

Hot-cross buns!
Hot-cross buns!
One a penny, two a penny,
Hot-cross buns!

Hot-cross buns!
Hot-cross buns!
If you have no daughters,
Give them to your sons.

161

Wooley Foster has gone to sea,
With silver buckles at his knee;
When he comes back he'll marry me.—
Bonny Wooley Foster!

Wooley Foster has a cow,
Black and white about the mow,
Open the gates and let her through,
Wooley Foster's ain cow!

Wooley Foster has a hen,
Cockle button, cockle ben,
She lay eggs for gentlemen,
But none for Wooley Foster!

162

The following catch is found in Ben Jonson's "Masque of Oberon", and is a most common nursery song at the present day.

Buz, quoth the blue fly,
Hum, quoth the bee,
Buz and hum they cry,
And so do we:
In his ear, in his nose,
Thus, do you see?
He ate the dormouse,
Else it was he.

163

As I was going up the hill,
I met with Jack the piper,
And all the tunes that he could play
Was "Tie up your petticoats tighter".
I tied them once, I tied them twice,
I tied them three times over;
And all the songs that he could sing
Was "Carry me safe to Dover".

164

There were two birds sat on a stone,
Fa, la, la, la, lal, de;
One flew away, and then there was one,
Fa, la, la, la, lal, de;
The other flew after, and then there was none,
Fa, la, la, la, lal, de;
And so the poor stone was left all alone,
Fa, la, la, la, lal, de!

165

How does my lady's garden grow?
How does my lady's garden grow?

With cockle shells, and silver bells,
And pretty maids all of a row.

166

There was a jolly miller
   Lived on the river Dee:
He worked and sung from morn till night,
   No lark so blithe as he;
And this the burden of his song
   For ever used to be—
I jump mejerrime jee!
   I care for nobody—no! not I,
Since nobody cares for me.

167

As I was going along, long, long,
A singing a comical song, song, song,
The lane that I went was so long, long, long,
And the song that I sung was as long, long, long,
And so I went singing along.

168

Where are you going, my pretty maid?
I'm going a-milking, sir, she said.
May I go with you, my pretty maid?
You're kindly welcome, sir, she said.
What is your father, my pretty maid?
My father's a farmer, sir, she said.
Say, will you marry me, my pretty maid?
Yes, if you please, kind sir, she said.
Will you be constant, my pretty maid?
That I can't promise you, sir, she said.
Then I won't marry you, my pretty maid!
Nobody asked you, sir! she said.

169

Song on the bells of Derby on foot-ball morning, a custom now discontinued.

> Pancakes and fritters,
> Say All Saints' and St Peter's;
> When will the *ball* come,
> Say the bells of St Alkmun;
> At two they will throw,
> Says Saint Werabo,
> O! very well,
> Says little Michel.

170

I have been to market, my lady, my lady;
Then you've not been to the fair, says pussy, says pussy.
I bought me a rabbit, my lady, my lady;
Then you did not buy a hare, says pussy, says pussy.
I roasted it, my lady, my lady;
Then you did not boil it, says pussy, says pussy;
I ate it, my lady, my lady;
And I'll eat you, says pussy, says pussy.

171

> My father left me three acres of land,
>   Sing ivy, sing ivy;
> My father left me three acres of land,
>   Sing holly, go whistle and ivy!
>
> I ploughed it with a ram's horn,
>   Sing ivy, sing ivy;
> And sowed it all over with one pepper corn,
>   Sing holly, go whistle and ivy!
>
> I harrowed it with a bramble bush,
>   Sing ivy, sing ivy;
> And reaped it with my little penknife,
>   Sing holly, go whistle and ivy!

I got the mice to carry it to the barn,
   Sing ivy, &c.
And threshed it with a goose's quill,
   Sing holly, &c.

I got the cat to carry it to the mill,
   Sing ivy, &c.
The miller he swore he would have her paw,
And the cat she swore she would scratch his face,
   Sing holly, go whistle and ivy!

172

The original of the following is to be found in "Deuteromelia,
or the second part of Músicks Melodie", 4to, Lond. 1609,
where the music is also given.

Three blind mice, see how they run!
They all ran after the farmer's wife,
Who cut off their tails with the carving-knife,
Did you ever see such fools in your life?
                      Three blind mice.

173

The music to the following song, with different words, is given
in "Melismata", 4to. Lond. 1611. See also the "Pills to Purge
Melancholy", 1719, vol. i. p. 14. The well-known song, "A
frog he would a wooing go", appears to have been borrowed
from this. See Dauney's "Ancient Scottish Melodies", 1838,
p. 53. The story is of old date, and in 1580 there was licensed
"A most strange weddinge of the frogge and the mouse", as
appears from the books of the Stationers' Company, quoted in
Warton's Hist. Engl. Poet, ed. 1840, vol. iii. p. 360.

There was a frog lived in a well,
   Kitty alone, Kitty alone;
There was a frog lived in a well,
   Kitty alone, and I!
There was a frog lived in a well,
   And a farce* mouse in a mill,
   Cock me cary, Kitty alone,
   Kitty alone, and I.

* Merry.

This frog he would a wooing ride,
   Kitty alone, &c.
This frog he would a wooing ride,
And on a snail he got astride,
   Cock me cary, &c.

He rode till he came to my Lady Mouse hall,
   Kitty alone, &c.
He rode till he came to my Lady Mouse hall,
And there he did both knock and call,
   Cock me cary, &c.

Quoth he, Miss Mouse, I'm come to thee,
   Kitty alone, &c.
Quoth he, Miss Mouse, I'm come to thee,
To see if thou canst fancy me,
   Cock me cary, &c.

Quoth she, answer I'll give you none,
   Kitty alone, &c.
Quoth she, answer I'll give you none,
Until my uncle Rat come home,
   Cock me cary, &c.

And when her uncle Rat came home,
   Kitty alone, &c.
And when her uncle Rat came home,
Who's been here since I've been gone?
   Cock me cary, &c.

Sir, there's been a worthy gentleman,
   Kitty alone, &c.
Sir, there's been a worthy gentleman,
That's been here since you've been gone,
   Cock me cary, &c.

The frog he came whistling through the brook,
   Kitty alone, &c.
The frog he came whistling through the brook.
And there he met with a dainty duck,
   Cock me cary, &c.

This duck she swallowed him up with a pluck,
   Kitty alone, Kitty alone;
This duck she swallowed him up with a pluck,
So there's an end of my history.
   Cock me cary, Kitty alone,
   Kitty alone, and I.

174

There was a man in our toone, in our toone, in our toone,
There was a man in our toone, and his name was Billy Pod;
And he played upon an old razor, an old razor, an old razor,
And he played upon an old razor, with my fiddle fiddle fe fum fo.

And his hat it was made of the good roast beef, the good roast beef,
   the good roast beef.
And his hat it was made of the good roast beef, and his name was
   Billy Pod;
And he played upon an old razor, &c.

And his coat it was made of the good fat tripe, the good fat tripe,
   the good fat tripe,
And his coat it was made of the good fat tripe, and his name was
   Billy Pod;
And he played upon an old razor, &c.

And his breeks were made of the bawbie baps, the bawbie baps, the
   bawbie baps,
And his breeks were made of the bawbie baps, and his name was
   Billy Pod;
And he played upon an old razor, &c.

And there was a man in tither toone, in tither toone, in tither toone,
And there was a man in tither toone, and his name was Edrin Drum;
And he played upon an old laadle, an old laadle, an old laadle,
And he played upon an old laadle, with my fiddle, fiddle fum fo.

And he ate up all the good roast beef, the good roast beef, &c. &c.
And he ate up all the good fat tripe, the good fat tripe, &c. &c.
And he ate up all the bawbie baps, &c., and his name was Edrin
   Drum.

175

John Cook had a little grey mare; he, haw, hum!
Her back stood up, and her bones they were bare; he, haw, hum!

John Cook was riding up Shuter's bank; he, haw, hum!
And there his nag did kick and prank; he, haw, hum!

John Cook was riding up Shuter's hill; he, haw, hum!
His mare fell down, and she made her will; he, haw, hum!

The bridle and saddle were laid on the shelf; he, haw, hum!
If you want any more you may sing it yourself; he, haw, hum!

176

A carrion crow sat on an oak,
  Fol de riddle, lol de riddle, hi ding do,
Watching a tailor shape his cloak;
  Sing heigh ho, the carrion crow,
  Fol de riddle, lol de riddle, hi ding do.

Wife, bring me my old bent bow,
  Fol de riddle, lol de riddle, hi ding do,
That I may shoot yon carrion crow;
  Sing heigh ho, the carrion crow,
  Fol de riddle, lol de riddle, hi ding do.

The tailor he shot and missed his mark,
  Fol de riddle, lol de riddle, hi ding do;
And shot his own sow quite through the heart;
  Sing heigh ho, the carrion crow,
  Fol de riddle, lol de riddle, hi ding do.

Wife, bring brandy in a spoon;
  Fol de riddle, lol de riddle, hi ding do,
For our old sow is in a swoon;
  Sing heigh ho, the carrion crow,
  Fol de riddle, lol de riddle, hi ding do.

177

Another version from MS. Sloane, 1489, fol. 17, written in the time of Charles I.

Hic hoc, the carrion crow,
For I have shot something too low:
I have quite missed my mark,
And shot the poor sow to the heart;
Wife, bring treacle in a spoon,
Or else the poor sow's heart will down.

178

Song of a little boy while passing his hour of solitude in a corn-field.

Awa' birds, away!
Take a little, and leave a little,
And do not come again;
For if you do,
I will shoot you through,
And there is an end of you.

179

If I'd as much money as I could spend,
I never would cry old chairs to mend;
Old chairs to mend, old chairs to mend;
I never would cry old chairs to mend.

If I'd as much money as I could tell,
I never would cry old clothes to sell;
Old clothes to sell, old clothes to sell;
I never would cry old clothes to sell.

180

Whistle, daughter, whistle, whistle daughter dear;
I cannot whistle, mammy, I cannot whistle clear.
Whistle, daughter, whistle, whistle for a pound;
I cannot whistle, mammy, I cannot make a sound.

181

I'll sing you a song,
Though not very long,
Yet I think it as pretty as any;
Put your hand in your purse,
You'll never be worse,
And give the poor singer a penny.

182

Dame, get up and bake your pies,
Bake your pies, bake your pies;
Dame, get up and bake your pies,
On Christmas-day in the morning.

Dame, what makes your maidens lie,
Maidens lie, maidens lie;
Dame, what makes your maidens lie,
On Christmas-day in the morning?

Dame, what makes your ducks to die,
Ducks to die, ducks to die;
Dame, what makes your ducks to die,
On Christmas-day in the morning?

Their wings are cut and they cannot fly,
Cannot fly, cannot fly;
Their wings are cut and they cannot fly,
On Christmas-day in the morning.

SEVENTH CLASS

Riddles

183

Ann.

There was a girl in our towne,
Silk an' satin was her gowne,
Silk an' satin, gold an' velvet,
Guess her name, three times I've tell'd it.

184

A thorn.

I went to the wood and got it,
I sat me down and looked at it;
The more I looked at it the less I liked it,
And I brought it home because I couldn't help it.

185

Sunshine.

Hick-a-more, Hack-a-more,
On the king's kitchen-door;
All the king's horses,

And all the king's men,
Couldn't drive Hick-a-more, Hack-a-more,
Off the king's kitchen-door!

186

A pen.

When I was taken from the fair body,
    They then cut off my head,
    And thus my shape was altered;
It's I that make peace between king and king,
    And many a true lover glad:
All this I do and ten times more,
    And more I could do still,
But nothing can I do,
    Without my guider's will.

187

Snuff.

As I look'd out o' my chamber window
    I heard something fall;
I sent my maid to pick it up,
    But she couldn't pick it all.

188

A tobacco-pipe.

I went into my grandmother's garden,
And there I found a farthing.
I went into my next door neighbour's,
There I bought a pipkin and a popkin—
A slipkin and a slopkin,
A nailboard, a sailboard,
And all for a farthing.

189

Gloves.

As I was going o'er London Bridge,
I met a cart full of fingers and thumbs!

190

Made in London,
Sold at York,
Stops a bottle
And *is* a cork.

191

Ten and ten and twice eleven,
Take out six and put in seven;
Go to the green and fetch eighteen,
And drop one a coming.

192

A walnut.

As soft as silk, as white as milk,
As bitter as gall, a thick wall,
And a great coat covers me all.

193

A swarm of bees.

As I was going o'er Tipple Tine,
I met a flock of bonny swine;
  Some green-lapp'd,
  Some green-back'd;
They were the very bonniest swine
That e'er went over Tipple Tine.

194

An egg.

Humpty Dumpty lay in a beck,*
With all his sinews round his neck;
Forty doctors and forty wrights
Couldn't put Humpty Dumpty to rights!

* A brook.

195

A storm of wind.

Arthur O'Bower has broken his band,
He comes roaring up the land;—
The King of Scots, with all his power,
Cannot turn Arthur of the Bower!

196

Tobacco.

Make three-fourths of a cross,
And a circle complete;
And let two semicircles
On a perpendicular meet;
Next add a triangle
That stands on two feet;
Next two semicircles,
And a circle complete.

197

There was a king met a king
In a narrow lane;
Says this king to that king,
"Where have you been?"

"Oh! I've been a hunting
With my dog and my doe."
"Pray lend him to me,
That I may do so."

"There's the dog, *take* the dog."
"What's the dog's name?"
"I've told you already."
"Pray tell me again."

198

A plum-pudding.

Flour of England, fruit of Spain,
Met together in a shower of rain;
Put in a bag tied round with a string,
If you'll tell me this riddle, I'll give you a ring.

199

Every lady in this land
Has twenty nails upon each hand,
Five and twenty hands and feet,
All this is true without deceit.

200

Twelve pears hanging high,
Twelve knights riding by;
Each knight took a pear,
And yet left eleven there!

201

A star.

I have a little sister, they call her peep, peep;
She wades the waters deep, deep, deep;
She climbs the mountains high, high, high;
Poor little creature, she has but one eye.

202

A needle and thread.

Old Mother Twitchett had but one eye,
And a long tail which she let fly;
And every time she went over a gap,
She left a bit of her tail in a trap.

203

An egg.

> In marble walls as white as milk,
> Lined with a skin as soft as silk,
> Within a fountain crystal clear,
> A golden apple doth appear.
> No doors there are to this stronghold.
> Yet things break in and steal the gold.

204

A horse-shoer.

What shoe-maker makes shoes without leather,
With all the four elements put together?
    Fire and water, earth and air;
    Every customer has two pair.

205

Currants.

> Higgledy piggledy
>   Here we lie,
> Pick'd and pluck'd,
>   And put in a pie.
My first is snapping, snarling, growling,
My second's industrious, romping, and prowling.
> Higgledy piggledy
>   Here we lie,
> Pick'd and pluck'd,
>   And put in a pie.

206

Thomas a Tattamus took two Ts,
To tie two tups to two tall trees,
To frighten the terrible Thomas a Tattamus!
Tell me how many Ts there are in all THAT.

207

The man had one eye, and the tree two apples upon it.

There was a man who had no eyes,
He went abroad to view the skies;
He saw a tree with apples on it,
He took no apples off, yet left no apples on it.

208

Cleopatra.

The moon nine days old,
The next sign to cancer;
Pat rat without a tail;—
And now, sir, for your answer?

209

A candle.

Little Nancy Etticoat,
In a white petticoat,
    And a red nose;
The longer she stands,
The shorter she grows.

210

Pair of tongs.

Long legs, crooked thighs,
Little head and no eyes.

211

From MS. Sloane, 1489, fol. 16, written in the time of Charles I.

There were three sisters in a hall,
There came a knight amongst them all;
Good morrow, aunt, to the one,
Good morrow, aunt, to the other,

Good morrow, gentlewoman, to the third,
If you were my aunt,
As the other two be,
I would say good morrow,
Then, aunts, all three.

212

Isabel.

Congeal'd water and Cain's brother,
That was my lover's name, and no other.

213

Teeth and gums.

Thirty white horses upon a red hill,
Now they tramp, now they champ, now they stand still.

214

Coals.

Black we are, but much admired;
Men seek for us till they are tired.
We tire the horse, but comfort man:
Tell me this riddle if you can?

215

A star.

Higher than a house, higher than a tree;
Oh, whatever can that be?

216

An egg.

Humpty Dumpty sate on a wall,
Humpty Dumpty had a great fall;
Three score men and three score more
Cannot place Humpty Dumpty as he was before.

217

The allusion to Oliver Cromwell satisfactorily fixes the date of
the riddle to belong to the seventeenth century. The answer is,
a rainbow.

Purple, yellow, red, and green,
The king cannot reach it nor the queen;
Nor can old Noll, whose power's so great:
Tell me this riddle while I count eight.

218

Pease-porridge hot, pease-porridge cold,
Pease-porridge in the pot, nine days old.
Spell me *that* without a P,
And a clever scholar you will be.

219

As I was going o'er Westminster bridge,
I met with a Westminster scholar;
He pulled off his cap *an' drew* off his glove,
And wished me a very good morrow.
What is his name?

220

A chimney.

Black within, and red without;
Four corners round about.

221

There was a man rode through our town,
Grey Grizzle was his name,
His saddle-bow was gilt with gold,
Three times I've named his name.

97

222

A hedgehog.

As I went over Lincoln bridge
I met Mister Rusticap;
Pins and needles on his back,
A going to Thorney fair.

223

One leg is a leg of mutton; two legs, a man; three legs, a stool;
four legs, a dog.

Two legs sat upon three legs,
With one leg in his lap;
In comes four legs,
And runs away with one leg.
Up jumps two legs,
Catches up three legs,
Throws it after four legs,
And makes him bring back one leg.

224

A bed.

Formed long ago, yet made to-day,
Employed while others sleep;
What few would like to give away,
Nor any wish to keep.

225

A cinder-sifter.

A riddle, a riddle, as I suppose,
A hundred eyes, and never a nose.

226

A well.

As round as an apple, as deep as a cup,
And all the king's horses can't pull it up.

227

A cherry.

As I went through the garden gap,
Who should I meet but Dick Red-cap!
A stick in his hand, a stone in his throat,
If you'll tell me this riddle, I'll give you a groat.

228

Elizabeth, Elspeth, Betsy and Bess,
They all went together to seek a bird's nest:
They found a bird's nest with five eggs in,
They all took one, and left four in.

229

As I was going to St Ives,
I met a man with seven wives,
Every wife had seven sacks,
Every sack had seven cats,
Every cat had seven kits:
Kits, cats, sacks, and wives,
How many were there going to St Ives?

230

The holly tree.

Highty, tighty, paradighty clothed in green,
The king could not read it, no more could the queen;
They sent for a wise man out of the East,
Who said it had horns, but was not a beast!

231

See, see! what shall I see?
A horse's head where its tail should be.

232

A fire-brand with sparks on it.

As I was going o'er London bridge,
And peep'd through a nick,
I saw four and twenty ladies
Riding on a stick!

233

An icicle.

Lives in winter,
Dies in summer,
And grows with its root upwards!

234

When I went up sandy hill,
I met a sandy boy;
I cut his throat, I sucked his blood,
And left his skin a hanging-o.

235

I had a little castle upon the sea-side,
One half was water, the other was land;
I opened my little castle door, and guess what I found;
I found a fair lady with a cup in her hand.
The cup was gold, filled with wine;
Drink, fair lady, and thou shalt be mine!

236

Old father Greybeard,
Without tooth or tongue;
If you'll give me your finger,
I'll give you my thumb.

EIGHTH CLASS

Charms

237

Cushy cow bonny, let down thy milk,
And I will give thee a gown of silk;
A gown of silk and a silver tee,
If thou wilt let down thy milk to me.

238

Said to pips placed in the fire; a species of divination practised
by children.

If you love me, pop and fly;
If you hate me, lay and die.

239

The following, with a very slight variation, is found in Ben
Jonson's "Masque of Queen's", and it is singular to account for
its introduction into the modern nursery.

I went to the toad that lies under the wall,
I charmed him out, and he came at my call;
I scratch'd out the eyes of the owl before,
I tore the bat's wing, what would you have more?

240

A charm somewhat similar to the following may be seen in the "Townley Mysteries", p. 91. See a paper in the "Archaeologia", vol. xxvii. p. 253, by the Rev. Lancelot Sharpe, M.A. See also MS. Lansd. 231, fol. 114, and Ady's "Candle in the Dark", 4to, London, 1650, p. 58.

Matthew, Mark, Luke and John,
Guard the bed that I lay on!
Four corners to my bed,
Four angels round my head;
One to watch, one to pray,
And two to bear my soul away!

241

Ady, in his "Candle in the Dark", 4to, Lond. 1650, p. 59, says that this was a charm to make butter come from the churn. It was to be said thrice.

Come, butter, come,
Come, butter, come!
Peter stands at the gate,
Waiting for a butter'd cake;
Come, butter, come!

242

From Dr Wallis's "Grammatica Linguæ Anglicanæ". 12mo, Oxon, 1674, p. 164. This and the nine following are said to be certain cures for the hiccup if repeated in one breath.

When a Twister a twisting will twist him a twist;
For the twisting of his twist, he three times doth intwist;
But if one of the twines of the twist do untwist,
The twine that untwisteth, untwisteth the twist.

Untwirling the twine that untwisteth between,
He twirls, with the twister, the two in a twine:
Then twice having twisted the twines of the twine
He twisteth the twine he had twined in twain.

The twain that, in twining, before in the twine,
As twines were intwisted; he now doth untwine:
'Twixt the twain inter-twisting a twine more between,
He, twirling his twister, makes a twist of the twine.

243

A thatcher of Thatchwood went to Thatchet a thatching;
Did a thatcher of Thatchwood go to Thatchet a thatching?
If a thatcher of Thatchwood went to Thatchet a thatching,
Where's the thatching the thatcher of Thatchwood has thatch'd?

244

Sometimes "off a pewter plate" is added at the end of each line.

Peter Piper picked a peck of pickled pepper;
A peck of pickled pepper Peter Piper picked;
If Peter Piper picked a peck of pickled peper,
Where's the peck of pickled pepper Peter Piper picked?

245

My father he left me, just as he was able,
One bowl, one bottle, one label,
Two bowls, two bottles, two labels,
Three, &c. [*And so on ad lib. in one breath.*]

246

Robert Rowley rolled a round roll round,
A round roll Robert Rowley rolled round;
Where rolled the round roll Robert Rowley rolled round?

247

My grandmother sent me a new-fashioned three cornered cambric
country cut handkerchief. Not an old-fashioned three cornered
cambric country cut handkerchief, but a new-fashioned three
cornered cambric country cut handkerchief.

248

Three crooked cripples went through Cripplegate, and through Cripplegate went three crooked cripples.

249

Swan swam over the sea—
Swim, swan, swim;
Swan swam back again,
Well swam swan.

250

Hickup, hickup, go away!
Come again another day;
Hickup, hickup, when I bake,
I'll give to you a butter-cake.

251

Hickup, snicup,
Rise up, right up!
Three drops in the cup,
Are good for the hiccup.

NINCH CLASS

Gaffers and Gammers

252

There was an old woman, as I've heard tell,
She went to market her eggs for to sell;
She went to market all on a market-day,
And she fell asleep on the king's highway.

There came by a pedlar, whose name was Stout,
He cut her petticoats all round about;
He cut her petticoats up to the knees,
Which made the old woman to shiver and freeze.

When this little woman first did wake,
She began to shiver and she began to shake,
She began to wonder and she began to cry,
"Oh! deary, deary me, this is none of I!"

"But if it be I, as I do hope it be,
I've a little dog at home, and he'll know me;
If it be I, he'll wag his little tail,
And if it be not I, he'll loudly bark and wail."

Home went the little woman all in the dark,
Up got the little dog, and he began to bark;
He began to bark, so she began to cry,
"Oh! deary, deary me, this is none of I!"

253

There was an old woman who lived in a shoe,
She had so many children she didn't know what to do;
She gave them some broth without any bread,
She whipped them all well and put them to bed.

254

Old woman, old woman, shall we go a shearing?
Speak a little louder, sir, I am very thick of hearing.
Old woman, old woman, shall I love you dearly?
Thank you, kind sir, I hear you very clearly.

255

There was an old woman sat spinning,
And that's the first beginning;
  She had a calf,
  And that's half;
She took it by the tail,
And threw it over the wall,
And that's all.

256

There was an old woman, her name it was Peg;
Her head was of wood, and she wore a cork-leg.
The neighbours all pitch'd her into the water,
Her leg was drown'd first, and her head follow'd a'ter.

257

A little old man and I fell out;
How shall we bring this matter about?
Bring it about as well as you can,
Get you gone, you little old man!

258

There was an old woman,
And she sold puddings and pies:
She went to the mill,
And the dust flew in her eyes:
Hot pies and cold pies to sell!
Wherever she goes,—
You may follow her by the smell.

259

Old Mother Niddity Nod swore by the pudding-bag,
She would go to Stoken Church fair;
And then old Father Peter said he would meet her
Before she got half-way there.

260

There was an old woman
Lived under a hill;
And if she's not gone,
She lives there still.

261

There was an old woman toss'd up in a basket
Nineteen times as high as the moon;
Where she was going I couldn't but ask it,
For in her hand she carried a broom.

Old woman, old woman, old woman, quoth I,
  O whither, O whither, O whither, so high?
To brush the cobwebs off the sky!
  Shall I go with thee? Ay, by and by.

262

There was an old man who liv'd in Middle Row,
He had five hens and a name for them, oh!
  Bill and Ned and Battock,
  Cut-her-foot and Pattock,
  Chuck, my lady Prattock,
Go to thy nest and lay.

263

There was an old woman of Leeds
Who spent all her time in good deeds;
  She worked for the poor
  Till her fingers were sore,
This pious old woman of Leeds!

264

Old Betty Blue
Lost a holiday shoe,
What can old Betty do?
Give her another
To match the other,
And then she may swagger in two.

265

Old mother Hubbard
Went to the cupboard,
To get her poor dog a bone:
But when she came there
The cupboard was bare,
And so the poor dog had none.

She went to the baker's
  To buy him some bread,
But when she came back
  The poor dog was dead.

She went to the joiner's
  To buy him a coffin,
But when she came back
  The poor dog was laughing.*

She took a clean dish
  To get him some tripe,
But when she came back
  He was smoking his pipe.

She went to the fishmonger's
  To buy him some fish,
And when she came back
  He was licking the dish.

She went to the ale-house
  To get him some beer,
But when she came back
  The dog sat in a chair.

She went to the tavern
  For white wine and red,
But when she came back
  The dog stood on his head.

She went to the hatter's
  To buy him a hat,
But when she came back
  He was feeding the cat.

She went to the barber's
  To buy him a wig,
But when she came back
  He was dancing a jig.

---

* Probably *loffing* or *loffin*, to complete the rhyme. So in
Shakespeare's "Mids. Night's Dream", Act ii. sc. 1: "And
then the whole quire hold their hips, and *loffe*."

She went to the fruiterer's
  To buy him some fruit,
But when she came back
  He was playing the flute.

She went to the tailor's
  To buy him a coat,
But when she came back
  He was riding a goat.

She went to the cobbler's
  To buy him some shoes,
But when she came back
  He was reading the news.

She went to the sempstress
  To buy him some linen,
But when she came back
  The dog was spinning.

She went to the hosier's
  To buy him some hose,
But when she came back
  He was dress'd in his clothes.

The dame made a curtsey,
  The dog made a bow;
The dame said, "your servant,"
  The dog said, "bow, wow."

266

The first two lines of the following are the same with those of
a song in D'Urfey's "Pills to Purge Melancholy", vol. v. p. 13.

There was an old woman
  Lived under a hill,
She put a mouse in a bag,
  And sent it to mill;

The miller declar'd
   By the point of his knife,
He never took toll
   Of a mouse in his life.

267

The following is part of a comic song called "Success to the Whistle and Wig", intended to be sung in rotation by the members of a club.

There was an old woman had three sons,
Jerry, and James, and John:
Jerry was hung, James was drowned,
John was lost and never was found,
And there was an end of the three sons,
Jerry, and James, and John!

268

The tale on which the following story is founded is found in a MS. of the fifteenth century, preserved in the Chetham Library at Manchester.

There was an old man, who lived in a wood,
   As you may plainly see;
He said he could do as much work in a day,
   As his wife could do in three.
With all my heart, the old woman said,
   If that you will allow,
To-morrow you'll stay at home in my stead,
   And I'll go drive the plough:

But you must milk the Tidy cow,
   For fear that she go dry;
And you must feed the little pigs
   That are within the sty;
And you must mind the speckled hen,
   For fear she lay away;

And you must reel the spool of yarn
  That I spun yesterday.

The old woman took a staff in her hand,
  And went to drive the plough:
The old man took a pail in his hand,
  And went to milk the cow;
But Tidy hinched, and Tidy flinched,
  And Tidy broke his nose,
And Tidy gave him such a blow,
  That the blood ran down to his toes.

High! Tidy! ho! Tidy! high!
  Tidy! do stand still;
If ever I milk you, Tidy, again,
  'Twill be sore against my will!

He went to feed the little pigs,
  That were within the sty;
He hit his head against the beam,
  And he made the blood to fly.
He went to mind the speckled hen,
  For fear she'd lay astray,
And he forgot the spool of yarn
  His wife spun yesterday.

So he swore by the sun, the moon, and the stars,
  And the green leaves on the tree,
If his wife didn't do a day's work in her life,
  She should ne'er be ruled by he.

269

There was an old man of Tobago,
Who lived on rice, gruel, and sago;
    Till, much to his bliss,
    His physician said this—
"To a leg, sir, of mutton you may go."

270

Oh, dear, what can the matter be?
Two old women got up in an apple-tree;
One came down,
And the other staid till Saturday.

271

There was an old man,
And he had a calf,
 And that's half;
He took him out of the stall,
And put him on the wall;
 And that's all.

272

Father Short came down the lane,
 Oh! I'm obliged to hammer and smite
 From four in the morning till eight at night,
For a bad master, and a worse dame.

273

There was an old woman call'd Nothing-at-all,
Who rejoiced in a dwelling exceedingly small:
A man stretched his mouth to its utmost extent,
And down at one gulp house and old woman went.

274

There was an old woman at Norwich,
Who lived upon nothing but porridge;
 Parading the town,
 She turned cloak into gown,
This thrifty old woman of Norwich.

275

A little old man of Derby,
How do you think he served me?
He took away my bread and cheese,
And that is how he served me.

276

There was an old woman in Surrey,
Who was morn, noon, and night in a hurry;
Called her husband a fool.
Drove the children to school,
The worrying old woman of Surrey.

Games

277

Rhymes used by children to decide who is to begin a game.

One-ery, two-ery,
    Ziccary zan;
Hollow bone, crack a bone,
    Ninery, ten;
Spittery spot,
    It must be done;
Twiddleum twaddleum,
    Twenty-one.

Hink spink, the puddings stink,
    The fat begins to fry,
Nobody at home, but jumping Joan,
    Father, mother, and I.
Stick, stock, stone dead,
    Blind man can't see,
Every knave will have a slave,
    You or I must be he.

278

A game of the Fox. In a children's game, where all the little actors are seated in a circle, the following stanza is used as question and answer.

Who goes round my house this night?
    None but cruel Tom:
Who steals all the sheep at night?
    None but this poor one.

279

Dance, Thumbkin, dance,
    [*Keep the thumb in motion.*
Dance, ye merry men, every one:
    [*All the fingers in motion.*
For Thumbkin, he can dance alone,
    [*The thumb only moving.*
Thumbkin, he can dance alone,
    [*Ditto.*
Dance, Foreman, dance,
    [*The first finger moving.*
Dance ye merrymen, every one;
    [*The whole moving.*
But Foreman, he can dance alone,
Foreman, he can dance alone.

And so on with the others—naming the 2d finger *Longman*—the 3d finger *Ringman* and the 4th finger *Littleman*. Littleman cannot dance alone.

280

The following is used by schoolboys, when two are starting to run a race.

One to make ready,
    And two to prepare;
Good luck to the rider,
    And away goes the mare.

281

At the conclusion, the captive is privately asked if he will have
oranges or lemons (the two leaders of the arch have previously
agreed which designation shall belong to each), and he goes behind the one he may chance to name. When all are thus divided
into two parties, they conclude the game by trying to pull each
other beyond a certain line.

Gay go up, and gay go down,
To ring the bells of London town.

Bull's eyes and targets,
Say the bells of St Marg'ret's.

Brickbats and tiles,
Say the bells of St Giles'.

Halfpence and farthings,
Say the bells of St Martin's.

Oranges and lemons,
Say the bells of St Clement's.

Pancakes and fritters,
Say the bells of St Peter's.

Two sticks and an apple,
Say the bells at Whitechapel.

Old Father Baldpate,
Say the slow bells at Aldgate.

You owe me ten shillings,
Say the bells at St Helen's.

Pokers and tongs,
Say the bells at St John's.

Kettles and pans,
Say the bells at St Ann's.

When will you pay me?
Say the bells at Old Bailey.

When I grow rich,
Say the bells at Shoreditch.

Pray when will that be?
Say the bells at Stepney.

I am sure I don't know,
Says the great bell at Bow.

Here comes a candle to light you to bed,
And here comes a chopper to chop off your head.

282

One child holds a wand to the face of another, repeating these
lines, and making grimaces, to cause the latter to laugh, and so
to the others; those who laugh paying a forfeit.

Buff says Buff to all his men,
And I say Buff to you again;
Buff neither laughs nor smiles,
But carries his face
With a very good grace,
And passes the stick to the very next place!

283

Game with the hands.

Pease-pudding hot,
Pease-pudding cold,
Pease-pudding in the pot,
Nine days old.
Some like it hot,
Some like it cold,
Some like it in the pot
Nine days old.

284

Awake, arise, pull out your eyes,
   And hear what time of day;
And when you have done, pull out your tongue,
   And see what you can say.

285

GAME OF THE GIPSY

One child is selected for Gipsy, one for Mother, and one for
Daughter Sue. The Mother says,

> I charge my daughters every one
> To keep good house while I am gone.
> You and *you* (*points*) but specially *you*,
> [*Or sometimes*, but specially *Sue*.]
> Or else I'll beat you black and blue.

During the Mother's absence, the Gipsy comes in, entices a
child away, and hides her. This process is repeated till all the
children are hidden, when the Mother has to find them.

286

This game begins thus: Take this—What's this?—A gaping,
wide-mouthed, waddling frog, &c.

Twelve huntsmen with horns and hounds,
Hunting over other men's grounds!
Eleven ships sailing o'er the main,
Some bound for France and some for Spain:
I wish them all safe home again:
Ten comets in the sky,
Some low and some high;
Nine peacocks in the air,
I wonder how they all come there,
I do not know, and I do not care;
Eight joiners in joiner's hall,
Working with the tools and all;

Seven lobsters in a dish,
As fresh as any heart could wish;
Six beetles against the wall,
Close by an old woman's apple stall;
Five puppies of our dog Ball,
Who daily for their breakfast call;
Four horses stuck in a bog.
Three monkeys tied to a clog;
Two pudding-ends would choke a dog,
With a gaping, wide-mouthed, waddling frog.

287

A string of children, hand in hand, stand in a row. A child (A) stands in front of them, as leader; two other children (B and C) form an arch, each holding both the hands of the other.

A. Draw a pail of water,
   For my lady's daughter;
   My father's a king, and my mother's a queen,
   My two little sisters are dress'd in green,
   Stamping grass and parsley,
   Marigold leaves and daisies.
B. One rush, two rush,
   Pray thee, fine lady, come under my bush.

A passes by under the arch, followed by the whole string of children, the last of whom is taken captive by B and C. The verses are repeated, until all are taken.

288

The following seems to belong to the last game; but it is usually found by itself in the small books of children's rhymes.

Sieve my lady's oatmeal,
   Grind my lady's flour,
Put it in a chestnut,
   Let it stand an hour;
One may rush, two may rush,
Come, my girls, walk under the bush.

289

Queen Anne, queen Anne, you sit in the sun,
As fair as a lily, as white as a wand.
I send you three letters, and pray read one,
You must read one, if you can't read all,
So pray, Miss or Master, throw up the ball.

290

There were three jovial Welshmen,
　　As I have heard them say,
And they would go a-hunting
　　Upon St David's day.

All the day they hunted,
　　And nothing could they find
But a ship a-sailing,
　　A-sailing with the wind.

One said it was a ship,
　　The other he said, nay;
The third said it was a house,
　　With the chimney blown away.

And all the night they hunted,
　　And nothing could they find
But the moon a-gliding,
　　A-gliding with the wind.

One said it was the moon, ·
　　The other he said, nay;
The third said it was a cheese,
　　And half o't cut away.

And all the day they hunted,
　　And nothing could they find
But a hedgehog in a bramble bush,
　　And that they left behind.

The first said it was a hedgehog,
   The second he said, nay;
The third it was a pincushion,
   And the pins stuck in wrong way.

And all the night they hunted,
   And nothing could they find
But a hare in a turnip field,
   And that they left behind.

The first said it was a hare,
   The second he said, nay;
The third said it was a calf,
   And the cow had run away.

And all the day they hunted,
   And nothing could they find
But an owl in a holly tree,
   And that they left behind.

One said it was an owl,
   The other he said, nay,
The third said 'twas an old man,
   And his beard growing grey.

291

Is John Smith within?—
Yes, that he is.
Can he set a shoe?—
Ay, marry, two,
Here a nail, there a nail,
Tick, tack, too.

292

Margery Mutton-pie, and Johnny Bopeep,
They met together in Gracechurch Street;
In and out, in and out, over the way,
Oh! says Johnny, 'tis chop-nose day.

293

Intery, mintery, cutery-corn,
Apple seed and apple thorn;
Wine, brier, limber-lock,
Five geese in a flock,
Sit and sing by a spring,
O-u-t, and in again.

294

The game of water-skimming is of high antiquity, being mentioned by Julius Pollux, and also by Eustathius in his commentary upon Homer. Brand quotes a curious passage from Minucius
Felix; but all antiquaries seem to have overlooked the very
curious notice in Higgins's adaptation of Junius's "Nomencla-
tor", 8vo, London, 1585, p. 299, where it is called "a duck and
a drake, and a halfe-penie cake". Thus it is probable that lines
like the following were employed in this game as early as 1585;
and it may be that the last line has recently furnished a hint to
Matthews in his amusing song in "Patter v. Clatter".

A duck and a drake,
A nice barley-cake,
With a penny to pay the old baker;
A hop and a scotch,
Is another notch,
Slitherum, slatherum, take her.

295

See, saw, Margery Daw,
Sold her bed and lay upon straw;
Was not she a dirty slut,
To sell her bed and lie in the dirt!

296

See, saw, Margery Daw,
Little Jackey shall have a new master;

Little Jackey shall have but a penny a day,
Because he can't work any faster.

297

1. I am a gold lock;
2. I am a gold key.
1. I am a silver lock;
2. I am a silver key.
1. I am a brass lock;
2. I am a brass key.
1. I am a lead lock;
2. I am a lead key.
1. I am a monk lock;
2. I am a monk key!

298

Ride a cock-horse to Banbury cross,
To buy little Johnny a galloping horse;
It trots behind and it ambles before,
And Johnny shall ride till he can ride no more.

299

Ride a cock-horse to Banbury-cross,
    To see what Tommy can buy;
A penny white loaf, a penny white cake,
    And a twopenny apple-pie.

300

Jack be nimble,
And Jack be quick:
And Jack jump over
The candlestick.

301

This should be accompanied by a kind of pantomimic dance, in which the motions of the body and arms express the process of weaving; the motion of the shuttle, &c.

Weave the diaper tick-a-tick tick,
Weave the diaper tick—
　Come this way, come that
　As close as a mat,
Athwart and across, up and down, round about,
And forwards, and backwards, and inside, and out;
Weave the diaper thick-a-thick thick,
Weave the diaper thick.

302

Used in Somersetshire in cutting out the game of pee-wip or pee-wit.

　　One-ery, two-ery, hickary, hum,
　　Fillison, follison, Nicholson, John,
　　Quever, quauver, Irish Mary,
　　Stenkarum, stankarum, buck!

303

　　Whoop, whoop, and hollow,
　　Good dogs won't follow,
　　Without the hare cries "pee wit."

304

Tom Brown's two little Indian boys,
　　One ran away,
　　The other wouldn't stay,—
Tom Brown's two little Indian boys.

305

　　There were two blackbirds,
　　　Sitting on a hill,

 The one named Jack,
  The other named Jill;
 Fly away, Jack!
 Fly away, Jill!
 Come again, Jack!
 Come again, Jill!

306

 Tip, top, tower,
 Tumble down in an hour.

307

1. I went up one pair of stairs,
2. Just like me.
1. I went up two pair of stairs;
2. Just like me.
1. I went into a room;
2. Just like me.
1. I looked out of a window;
2. Just like me.
1. And there I saw a monkey;
2. Just like me.

308

Number number nine, this hoop's mine;
Number number ten, take it back again.

309

 Here goes my lord,
A trot, a trot, a trot, a trot;
 Here goes my lady,
A canter, a canter, a canter, a canter!
 Here goes my young master,
Jockey-hitch, Jockey-hitch, Jockey-hitch, Jockey-hitch!

Here goes my young miss,
An amble, an amble, an amble, an amble!
The footman lags behind to tipple ale and wine,
And goes gallop, a gallop, a gallop, to make up his time.

310

This is acted by two or more girls, who walk or dance up and down, turning, when they say, "turn, cheeses, turn". The "green cheeses", as I am informed, are made with sage and potato-tops. Two girls are said to be "cheese and cheese".

Green cheese, yellow laces,
Up and down the market-places,
Turn, cheeses, turn!

311

To market ride the gentlemen,
So do we, so do we!
Then comes the country clown,
Hobbledy gee, hobbledy gee;
First go the ladies, nim, nim, nim:
Next come the gentlemen, trim, trim, trim;
Then come the country clowns, gallop-a-trot.

312

Ride a cock-horse to Coventry cross,
To see what Emma can buy;
A penny white cake I'll buy for her sake,
And a twopenny tart or a pie.

313

Ride a cock-horse to Banbury cross,
To see an old lady upon a white horse,
Rings on her fingers, and bells on her toes,
And so she makes music wherever she goes.

314

Song set to five toes.

   1. Let us go to the wood, says this pig;
   2. What to do there? says that pig;
   3. To look for my mother, says this pig;
   4. What to do with her? says that pig;
   5. Kiss her to death, says this pig.

315

A number of boys and girls stand round one in the middle, who repeats the following lines, counting the children until one is counted out by the end of the verses.

Ring me (1), ring me (2), ring me rary (3),
As I go round (4), ring by ring (5),
A virgin (6) goes a maying (7),
Here's a flower (8), and there's a flower (9),
Growing in my lady's garden (10),
If you set your foot awry (11),
Gentle John will make you cry (12),
If you set your foot amiss (13),
Gentle John (14) will give you a kiss.

The child upon whom (14) falls is then taken out, and forced to select one of the other sex. The middle child then proceeds.

This [lady or gentleman] is none of ours,
Has put [him or her] self in [the selected child's] power,
So clap all hands, and ring all bells, and make the wedding o'er.
                                      [All clap hands.]

If the child taken by lot joins in the clapping, the selected child is rejected and I believe takes the middle place. Otherwise, I think, there is a salute.

316

Another game, played, exclusively by boys. Two, who are fixed upon for the purpose, leave the group, and privately arrange that the pass-word shall be some implement of a particular trade. The trade is announced in the dialogue, and then the fun is, that the unfortunate wight who guesses the "tool" is beaten with the caps of his fellows till he reaches a fixed goal, after which he goes out in turn.

"Two broken tradesmen,
　　Newly come over,
The one from France and Scotland,
　　The other from Dover."
"What's your trade?"

Carpenters, nailors, smiths, tinkers, or any other is answered; and on guessing the instrument "plane him, hammer him, rasp him, or solder him", is called out respectively during the period of punishment.

317

Clap hands, clap hands,
　　Hie Tommy Randy,
Did you see my good man?
　　They call him Cock-a-bandy.

Silken stockings on his legs,
　　Silver buckles glancin',
A sky-blue bonnet on his head,
　　And oh, but he is handsome.

318

A song set to five fingers.

1. This pig went to market;
2. This pig stayed at home;
3. This pig had a bit of meat;
4. And this pig had none;
5. This pig said, Wee, wee, wee!
　　I can't find my way home.

319

Children hunting bats.

Bat, bat, (*clap hands,*)
　　Come under my hat,
And I'll give you a slice of bacon;

And when I bake,
I'll give you a cake,
If I am not mistaken.

320

A game at ball.

> Cuckoo, cherry-tree,
> Catch a bird, and give it to me;
> Let the tree be high or low,
> Let it hail, rain, or snow.

321

Two of the strongest children are selected, A and B; A stands within a ring of the children, B being outside.

A. Who is going round my sheepfold?
B. Only poor old Jackey Lingo.
A. Don't steal any of my black sheep.
B. No, no more I will, only by one,
   Up, says Jackey Lingo.

(*Strikes one.*)

The child struck leaves the ring, and takes hold of B behind; B in the same manner takes the other children, one by one, gradually increasing his tail on each repetition of the verses, until he has got the whole: A then tries to get them back; B runs away with them; they try to shelter themselves behind B; A drags them off, one by one, setting them against a wall, until he has recovered all. A regular tearing game, as children say.

322

Highty cock O!
To London we go,
To York we ride;
And Edward has pussy-cat tied to his side;
He shall have little dog tied to the other,
And then he goes trid-trod to see his grandmother.

323

This is the key of the kingdom.
In that kingdom there is a city.
In that city there is a town.
In that town there is a street.
In that street there is a lane.
In that lane there is a yard.
In that yard there is a house.
In that house there is a room.
In that room there is a bed.
On that bed there is a basket.
In that basket there are some flowers.
Flowers in the basket, basket in the bed, bed in the room, &c, &c.

324

Children stand round, and are counted one by one, by means of this rhyme. The child upon whom the last number falls is *out*, for "Hide or Seek", or any other game where a victim is required. A cock and bull story of this kind is related of the historian Josephus. There are other versions of this, and one may be seen in "Blackwood's Magazine" for August, 1821, p. 36.

Hickory (1), Dickory (2), Dock (3),
The mouse ran up the clock (4),
The clock struck one (5),
The mouse was gone (6);
O (7), U (8), T (9), spells OUT!

325

One old Oxford ox opening oysters;
Two tee-totums totally tired of trying to trot to Tadbury;
Three tall tigers tippling tenpenny tea;
Four fat friars fanning fainting flies;
Five frippy Frenchmen foolishly fishing for flies;
Six sportsmen shooting snipes;

Seven Severn salmons swallowing shrimps;
Eight Englishmen eagerly examining Europe;
Nine nimble noblemen nibbling nonpareils;
Ten tinkers tinkling upon ten tin tinder-boxes with ten ten-
    penny tacks;
Eleven elephants elegantly equipt;
Twelve typographical topographers typically translating types.

326

The following lines are sung by children when starting for a race.

Good horses, bad horses,
    What is the time of day?
Three o'clock, four o'clock,
    Now fare you away.

327

See-saw, jack a daw,
What is a craw to do wi' her?
She has not a stocking to put on her,
And the craw has not one for to gi' her.

328

The following is a game played as follows: A string of boys and
girls, each holding by his predecessor's skirts, approaches two
others, who with joined and elevated hands form a double arch.
After the dialogue, the line passes through, and the last is
caught by a sudden lowering of the arms—if possible.

How many miles is it to Babylon?—
Threescore miles and ten.
Can I get there by candle-light?—
Yes, and back again!
If your heels are nimble and light,
You may get there by candle-light.

329

Clap hands, clap hands!
Till father comes home;
For father's got money,
But mother's got none.
Clap hands, &c.
Till father, &c.

330

See-saw sacradown,
Which is the way to London town?
One foot up, and the other down,
And that is the way to London town.

331

Here stands a post,
Who put it there?
A better man than you;
Touch it if you dare!

332

A stands with a row of girls (her daughters) behind her; B, a
suitor, advances.

B. Trip trap over the grass:
  If you please will you let one of your [eldest] daughters come,
Come and dance with me?
I will give you pots and pans, I will give you brass,
I will give you anything for a pretty lass.
A. says, "No."
B. I will give you gold and silver, I will give you pearl,
I will give you anything for a pretty girl.
A. Take one, take one, the fairest you may see.
B. The fairest one that I can see
Is pretty Nancy,—come to me.

[B carries one off, and says:]

You shall have a duck, my dear,
And you shall have a drake,
And you shall have a young man apprentice for your sake.

[Children say:]

If this young man should happen to die,
And leave this poor woman a widow,
The bells shall all ring, and the birds shall all sing,
And we'll all clap hands together.

So it is repeated until the whole are taken.

333

The "Three Knights of Spain" is a game played in nearly the same manner as the preceding. The *dramatis personæ* form themselves in two parties, one representing a courtly dame and her daughters, the other the suitors of the daughters. The last party, moving backwards and forwards, with their arms entwined, approach and recede from the mother party, which is stationary, singing to a very sweet air. See Chambers' "Popular Rhymes", p. 66.

Suitors

We are three brethren out of Spain,
Come to court your daughter Jane.

Mother

My daughter Jane she is too young,
And has not learned her mother tongue.

Suitors

Be she young, or be she old,
For her beauty she must be sold.
So fare you well, my lady gay,
We'll call again another day.

Mother

Turn back, turn back, thou scornful knight,
And rub thy spurs till they be bright.

Suitors

Of my spurs take you no thought,
For in this town they were not bought,
So fare you well, my lady gay,
We'll call again another day.

Mother

Turn back, turn back, thou scornful knight,
And take the fairest in your sight.

Suitor

The fairest maid that I can see,
Is pretty Nancy,—come to me.
Here comes your daughter safe and sound,
Every pocket with a thousand pound;
Every finger with a gay gold ring;
Please to take your daughter in.

334

A game on the slate.

Eggs, butter, bread,
Stick, stock, stone dead!
Stick him up, stick him down,
Stick him in the old man's crown!

335

In the following childish amusement, one extends his arm, and the other in illustration of the narrative, strikes him gently with the side of his hand at the shoulder and wrist; and then at the word "middle", with considerable force, on the flexor muscles at the elbow-joint.

My father was a Frenchman,
 He bought me for a fiddle,
He cut me here, he cut me here,
 He cut me right in the middle.

336

Patting the foot on the five toes.

> Shoe the colt, shoe!
>   Shoe the wild mare;
> Put a sack on her back,
>   See if she'll bear.
> If she'll bear,
>   We'll give her some grains;
> If she won't bear,
>   We'll dash out her brains!

337

Game on a child's features.

> Here sits the Lord Mayor,
>   *forehead.*
> Here sit his two men,
>   *eyes.*
> Here sits the cock,
>   *right cheek.*
> Here sits the hen,
>   *left cheek.*
> Here sit the little chickens,
>   *tip of nose.*
> Here they run in,
>   *mouth.*
> Chinchopper, chinchopper,
> Chinchopper, chin!
>   *chuck the chin.*

338

A play with the face. The child exclaims:

> Ring the bell!
>   *giving a lock of its hair a pull.*

Knock at the door!
> *tapping its forehead.*

Draw the latch!
> *pulling up its nose.*

And walk in!
> *opening its mouth and putting in its finger.*

339

An exercise during which the fingers of the child are enumer-
ated.

Thumbikin, Thumbikin, broke the barn,
Pinnikin, Pinnikin, stole the corn.
  Long back Gray
  Carried it away.
Old Mid-man sat and saw,
But Peesy-weesy paid for a'.

340

This pig went to market,
  Squeak mouse, mouse mousey;
Shoe, shoe, shoe the wild colt,
  And here's my own doll, Dowsy.

341

From Yorkshire. A game to alarm children.

Flowers, flowers, high-no!
Sheeny, greeny, rino!—
  Sheeny greeny,
  Sheeny greeny,
Rum tum fra!

342

1. This pig went to the barn,
2. This ate all the corn.
3. This said he would tell.
4. This said he wasn't well.
5. This went week, week, week, over the door sill.

343

The two following are fragments of a game called "The Lady of the Land", a complete version of which has not fallen in my way.

Here comes a poor woman from baby-land,
With three small children in her hand:
One can brew, the other can bake,
The other can make a pretty round cake.
One can sit in the garden and spin,
Another can make a fine bed for the king;
Pray, ma'am, will you take one in?

344

I can make diet bread,
Thick and thin;
I can make diet bread
Fit for the king.

345

Here we come a piping,
First in spring, and then in May;
The queen she sits upon the sand,
Fair as a lily, white as a wand:
King John has sent you letters three,
And begs you'll read them unto me.—
We can't read one without them all,
So pray, Miss Bridget, deliver the ball!

346

The first day of Christmas,
My true love sent to me
A partridge in a pear-tree.

The second day of Christmas,
My true love sent to me
Two turtle doves and
A partridge in a pear-tree.

The third day of Christmas,
My true love sent to me
Three French hens,
Two turtle doves, and
A partridge in a pear-tree.

The fourth day of Christmas,
My true love sent to me
Four colly birds,
Three French hens,
Two turtle doves, and
A partridge in a pear-tree.

The fifth day of Christmas,
My true love sent to me
Five gold rings,
Four colly birds,
Three French hens,
Two turtle doves, and
A partridge in a pear-tree.

The sixth day of Christmas,
My true love sent to me
Six geese a laying,
Five gold rings,
Four colly birds,
Three French hens,
Two turtle doves, and
A partridge in a pear-tree.

The seventh day of Christmas,
My true love sent to me
Seven swans a swimming,
Six geese a laying,
Five gold rings,
Four colly birds,
Three French hens,
Two turtle doves, and
A partridge in a pear-tree.

The eighth day of Christmas,
My true love sent to me
Eight maids a milking,
Seven swans a swimming,
Six geese a laying,
Five gold rings,
Four colly birds,
Three French hens,
Two turtle doves, and
A partridge in a pear-tree

The ninth day of Christmas,
My true love sent to me
Nine drummers drumming,
Eight maids a milking,
Seven swans a swimming,
Six geese a laying,
Five gold rings,
Four colly birds,
Three French hens,
Two turtle doves, and
A partridge in a pear-tree.

The tenth day of Christmas,
My true love sent to me
Ten pipers piping,
Nine drummers drumming,
Eight maids a milking,
Seven swans a swimming,

Six geese a laying,
Five gold rings,
Four colly birds,
Three French hens,
Two turtle doves, and
A partridge in a pear-tree.

The eleventh day of Christmas,
My true love sent to me
Eleven ladies dancing,
Ten pipers piping,
Nine drummers drumming,
Eight maids a milking,
Seven swans a swimming,
Six geese a laying,
Five gold rings,
Four colly birds,
Three French hens,
Two turtle doves, and
A partridge in a pear-tree.

The twelfth day of Christmas,
My true love sent to me
Twelve lords a leaping,
Eleven ladies dancing,
Ten pipers piping,
Nine drummers drumming,
Eight maids a milking,
Seven swans a swimming,
Six geese a laying,
Five gold rings.
Four colly birds,
Three French hens,
Two turtle doves, and
A partridge in a pear-tree.

Each child in succession repeats the gifts of the day, and for-
feits for each mistake. This accumulative process is a favourite
with children: in early writers, such as Homer, the repetition
of messages, &c., pleases on the same principle.

347

A game on the fingers.

> Heetum peetum penny pie,
> Populorum gingum gie;
> East, West, North, South,
> Kirby, Kendal, Cock him out!

348

A game-rhyme.

> Trip and go, heave and hoe,
> Up and down, to and fro;
> From the town to the grove
> Two and two let us rove,
> A-maying, a-playing;
> Love hath no gainsaying;
> So merrily trip and go.
> So merrily trip and go!

349

This is the way the ladies ride;
    Tri, tre, tre, tree,
    Tri, tre, tre, tree!
This is the way the ladies ride,
    Tri, tre, tre, tre, tri-tre-tre-tree!

This is the way the gentlemen ride;
    Gallop-a-trot,
    Gallop-a-trot!
This is the way the gentlemen ride,
    Gallop-a-gallop-a-trot!

This is the way the farmers ride;
    Hobbledy-hoy,
    Hobbledy-hoy!
This is the way the farmers ride;
    Hobbledy-hobbledy-hoy!

350

There was a man, and his name was Dob,
And he had a wife, and her name was Mob,
And he had a dog, and he called it Cob,
And she had a cat, called Chitterabob.
 Cob, says Dob,
 Chitterabob, says Mob,
 Cob was Dob's dog,
 Chitterabob Mob's cat.

351

Two children sit opposite to each other; the first turns her fingers one over the other, and says:

"May my geese fly over your barn?"

The other answers, Yes, if they'll do no harm. Upon which the first unpacks the fingers of her hand, and waving it over head, says:

"Fly over his barn and eat all his corn."

352

Now we dance looby, looby, looby,
Now we dance looby, looby, light,
Shake your right hand a little
And turn you round about.

Now we dance looby, looby, looby,
Shake your right hand a little,
Shake your left hand a little,
And turn you round about.

Now we dance lobby, looby, looby,
Shake your right hand a little,
Shake your left hand a little,
Shake your right foot a little,
And turn you round about.

Now we dance looby, looby, looby,
Shake your right hand a little,
Shake your left hand a little,
Shake your right foot a little,
Shake your left foot a little,
And turn you round about.

Now we dance looby, looby, looby,
Shake your right hand a little,
Shake your left hand a little,
Shake your right foot a little,
Shake your left foot a little,
Shake your head a little,
And turn you round about.

Children dance round first, then stop and shake the hand, &c.;
then turn slowly round, and then dance in a ring again.

353

THE OLD DAME

One child, called the Old Dame, sits on the floor, and the rest,
joining hands, form a circle round her, and dancing, sing the
following lines:

Children

To Beccles! to Beccles!
To buy a bunch of nettles!
Pray, old Dame, what's o'clock?

Dame

One, going for two.

Children

To Beccles! to Beccles!
To buy a bunch of nettles!
Pray, old Dame, what's o'clock?

Dame

Two, going for three.

And so on till she reaches, "Eleven going for twelve". After this
the following questions are asked, with the replies.—C. Where
have you been? D. To the wood. C. What for? D. To pick up
sticks. C. What for? D. To light my fire. C. What for? D. To
boil my kettle. C. What for? D. To cook some of your chickens.
—The children then all run away as fast as they can, and the
Old Dame tries to catch one of them. Whoever is caught is the
next to personate the Dame.

354

DROP GLOVE

Children stand round in a circle, leaving a space between each.
One walks round the outside, and carries a glove in her hand,
saying:

> I've a glove in my hand,
>> Hittity hot!
> Another in my other hand,
>> Hotter than that!
> So I sow beans and so they come up,
> Some in a mug, and some in a cup.
>> I sent a letter to my love,
>> I lost it, I lost it!
>> I found it, I found it!
>> It burns, it scalds.

Repeating the last words very rapidly, till she drops the glove
behind one of them, and whoever has the glove must overtake
her, following her exactly in and out till she catches her. If the
pursuer makes a mistake in the pursuit, she loses, and the game
is over; otherwise she continues the game with the glove.

355

In the following, the various parts of the countenance are
touched as the lines are repeated; and at the close the chin is
struck playfully, that the tongue may be gently bitten.

> Eye winker,
> Tom Tinker,
>> Nose dropper.
> Mouth eater,
> Chin chopper,
>> Chin chopper.

356

Thumb bold,
Thibity-thold,
Langman,
Lick pan,
Mamma's little man.

357

A game of the fox.

Fox a fox, a brummalary,
How many miles to Lummaflary? Lummabary.
A. Eight and eight, and a hundred and eight.
How shall I get home to-night?
A. Spin your legs and run fast.

358

A Christmas custom in Lancashire. The boys dress themselves
up with ribands, and perform various pantomimes, after which
one of them, who has a blackened face, a rough skin coat, and a
broom in his hand, sings as follows:

Here come I,
Little David Doubt;
If you don't give me money,
I'll sweep you all out.
Money I want,
And money I crave;
If you don't give me money,
I'll sweep you all to the grave!

359

The following lines are said by the nurse when moving the
child's foot up and down.

The dog of the kill,*
He went to the mill
To lick mill-dust:

* That is, kiln.

The miller he came
With a stick on his back—
Home, dog, home!
The foot behind,
The foot before:
When he came to a stile,
Thus he jumped o'er.

360

The following lines are repeated by the nurse when sliding her hand down the child's face.

My mother and your mother
Went over the way;
Said my mother to your mother,
It's chop-a-nose day!

ELEVENTH CLASS

Paradoxes

361

The following is quoted in Parkin's reply to Dr Stukeley's second number of "Origines Roystonianæ", 4to, London, 1748, p. vi.

> Peter White will ne'er go right,
>   Would you know the reason why?
> He follows his nose where'er he goes,
>   And that stands all awry.

362

> O that I was where I would be,
> Then would I be where I am not.
> But where I am I must be,
> And where I would be I cannot.

363

The following was sung to the tune of Chevy Chase. It was taken from a poetical tale in the "Choyce Poems", 12mo, London, 1662, the music to which may be seen in D'Urfey's "Pills to Purge Melancholy", 1719, vol. iv. p. 1.

Three children sliding on the ice
   Upon a summer's day,
As it fell out, they all fell in,
   The rest they ran away.

Now had these children been at home,
   Or sliding on dry ground,
Ten thousand pounds to one penny
   They had not all been drown'd.

You parents all that children have,
   And you that have got none,
If you would have them safe abroad,
   Pray keep them safe at home.

364

There was a man of Newington,
   And he was wond'rous wise,
He jump'd into a quickset hedge,
   And scratch'd out both his eyes:
But when he saw his eyes were out,
   With all his might and main
He jump'd into another hedge,
   And scratch'd 'em in again.

365

Up stairs, down stairs, upon my lady's window,
There I saw a cup of sack and a race of ginger;
Apples at the fire, and nuts to crack,
A little boy in the cream-pot up to his neck.

366

I would if I cou'd,
If I cou'dn't, how cou'd I?
I cou'dn't, without I cou'd, cou'd I?

Cou'd you, without you cou'd, cou'd ye?
Cou'd ye, cou'd ye?
Cou'd you, without you cou'd, cou'd ye?

367

If all the world was apple pie,
   And all the sea was ink,
And all the trees were bread and cheese,
   What should we have for drink?

368

Tobacco wick! tobacco wick!
When you're well, 'twill make you sick;
Tobacco wick! tobacco wick!
'Twill make you well when you are sick.

369

The following occurs in a MS. of the seventeenth century, in
the Sloane Collection, the reference to which I have mislaid.

The man in the wilderness asked me,
How many strawberries grew in the sea?
I answered him, as I thought good,
As many as red herrings grew in the wood.

370

The conclusion of the following resembles a verse in the nursery
history of Mother Hubbard.

There was an old woman, and what do you think?
She lived upon nothing but victuals and drink:
Victuals and drink were the chief of her diet:
This tiresome old woman could never be quiet.

She went to the baker to buy her some bread,
And when she came home her old husband was dead;
She went to the clerk to toll the bell,
And when she came back her old husband was well.

371

Here am I, little jumping Joan;
When nobody's with me
I'm always alone.

372

There was an old woman had nothing,
And there came thieves to rob her;
When she cried out she made no noise,
But all the country heard her.

373

There was a little guinea-pig,
Who, being little, was not big,
He always walked upon his feet,
And never fasted when he ate.

When from a place he ran away,
He never at that place did stay;
And while he ran, as I am told,
He ne'er stood still for young or old.

He often squeak'd and sometimes vi'lent,
And when he squeak'd he ne'er was silent;
Though ne'er instructed by a cat,
He knew a mouse was not a rat.

One day, as I am certified,
He took a whim and fairly died;
And, as I'm told by men of sense,
He never has been living since.

374

Mind your punctuation!

I saw a peacock with a fiery tail,
I saw a blazing comet drop down hail,
I saw a cloud wrapped with ivy round,
I saw an oak creep upon the ground,
I saw a pismire swallow up a whale,
I saw the sea brimful of ale,
I saw a Venice glass full fifteen feet deep,
I saw a well full of men's tears that weep,
I saw red eyes all of a flaming fire,
I saw a house bigger than the moon and higher,
I saw the sun at twelve o'clock at night,
I saw the man that saw this wondrous sight.

375

My true love lives far from me,
    Perrie, Merrie, Dixie, Dominie.
Many a rich present he sends to me,
      Petrum, Partrum, Paradise, Temporie,
    Perrie, Merrie, Dixie, Dominie.

He sent me a goose without a bone;
He sent me a cherry without a stone.
    Petrum, &c.

He sent me a Bible, no man could read;
He sent me a blanket, without a thread.
    Petrum, &c.

How could there be a goose without a bone?
How could there be a cherry without a stone?
    Petrum, &c.

How could there be a Bible no man could read?
How could there be a blanket without a thread?
    Petrum, &c.

When the goose is in the eggshell, there is no bone;
When the cherry is in the blossom, there is no stone.
    Petrum, &c.

When ye Bible is in ye press no man it can read;
When ye wool is on ye sheep's back, there is no thread.
    Petrum, &c.

376

There was a man and he was mad,
And he jump'd into a pea-swad;*
The pea-swad was over-full,
So he jump'd into a roaring bull;
The roaring bull was over-fat,
So he jump'd into a gentleman's hat;
The gentleman's hat was over fine,
So he jump'd into a bottle of wine;
The bottle of wine was over-dear,
So he jump'd into a bottle of beer;
The bottle of beer was over-thick,
So he jump'd into a club-stick;
The club-stick was over narrow,
So he jump'd into a wheel-barrow;
The wheel-barrow began to crack,
So he jump'd on to a hay-stack;
The hay-stack began to blaze,
So he did nothing but cough and sneeze!

* The pod or shell of a pea.

377

I saw a ship a-sailing
  A-sailing on the sea;
And, oh! it was all laden
  With pretty things for thee!

There were comfits in the cabin,
   And apples in the hold;
The sails were made of silk,
   And the masts were made of gold:

The four-and-twenty sailors
   That stood between the decks,
Were four-and-twenty white mice,
   With chains about their necks.

The captain was a duck,
   With a packet on his back;
And when the ship began to move,
   The captain said, "Quack! quack!"

378

   Barney Bodkin broke his nose,
   Without feet we can't have toes;
   Crazy folk are always mad,
   Want of money makes us sad.

379

If a man who turnips cries
Cries not when his father dies,
It is a proof that he would rather
Have a turnip than his father.

Lullabies

380

Hushy baby, my doll, I pray you don't cry,
And I'll give you some bread and some milk by and by;
Or, perhaps you like custard, or may-be a tart,—
Then to either you're welcome, with all my whole heart.

381

Dance, little baby, dance up high,
Never mind, baby, mother is by;
Crow and caper, caper and crow;
There, little baby, there you go;
Up to the ceiling, down to the ground,
Backwards and forwards, round and round;
Dance, little baby, and mother will sing,
With the merry coral, ding, ding, ding!

382

The following is quoted in Florio's "New World of Words",
fol., London, 1611 p. 3.

To market, to market,
To buy a plum bun;

Home again, come again,
Market is done.

383

Dance to your daddy,
My little babby,
Dance to your daddy,
My little lamb.

You shall have a fishy
In a little dishy;
You shall have a fishy
When the boat comes in.

384

Tom shall have a new bonnet,
With blue ribands to tie on it,
With a hush-a-by and a lull-a-baby,
Who so like to Tommy's daddy!

385

Bye, baby bumpkin,
Where's Tony Lumpkin?
My lady's on her death-bed
With eating half a pumpkin.

386

From "The Pleasant Comœdie of Patient Grissell," 1603.

Hush, hush, hush, hush!
And I dance mine own child,
And I dance mine own child,
Hush, hush, hush, hush!

387

Hush thee, my babby,
Lie still with thy daddy,
Thy mammy has gone to the mill,
To grind thee some wheat,
To make thee some meat,
And so, my dear babby, lie still.

388

Hey, my kitten, my kitten,
And hey, my kitten, my deary!
Such a sweet pet as this
Was neither far nor neary.

Here we go up, up, up,
And here we go down, down, downy;
And here we go backwards and forwards,
And here we go round, round, roundy.

389

I won't be my father's Jack,
I won't be my mother's Gill,
I will be the fiddler's wife,
And have music when I will.
T' other little tune,
T' other little tune,
Pr'ythee, love, play me
T' other little tune.

390

Danty baby diddy,
What can a mammy do wid'e,
But sit in a lap,
And give 'un a pap?
Sing danty baby diddy.

391

Rock-a-bye baby, thy cradle is green;
Father's a nobleman, mother's a queen;
And Betty's a lady, and wears a gold ring;
And Johnny's a drummer, and drums for the king.

392

Bye, O my baby!
When I was a lady,
O then my poor baby didn't cry!
But my baby is weeping,
For want of good keeping.
Oh, I fear my poor baby will die!

393

Hush-a-bye, a ba lamb,
Hush-a-bye a milk cow,
You shall have a little stick
To beat the naughty bow-wow.

394

Hush-a-bye baby, on the tree top,
When the wind blows, the cradle will rock;
When the bough bends, the cradle will fall.
Down will come baby, bough, cradle, and all.

395

Ride, baby, ride,
Pretty baby shall ride,
And have a little puppy-dog tied to her side,

And little pussy-cat tied to the other,
And away she shall ride to see her grandmother,
  To see her grandmother,
  To see her grandmother.

396

Bye, baby bunting,
Daddy's gone a hunting,
To get a little hare's skin
To wrap a baby bunting in.

397

Give me a blow, and I'll beat 'em,
  Why did they vex my baby?
Kissy, kiss, kissy, my honey,
  And cuddle your nurse, my deary.

398

My dear cockadoodle, my jewel, my joy,
My darling, my honey, my pretty sweet boy;
Before I do rock thee with soft lullaby,
Give me thy dear lips to be kiss'd, kiss'd, kiss'd.

399

A favourite lullaby in the north of England fifty years ago, and
perhaps still heard. The last word is pronounced *bee*.

Hush-a-bye, lie still and sleep,
It grieves me sore to see thee weep,
For when thou weep'st thou wearies me,
Hush-a-bye, lie still and *bye*.

400

From Yorkshire and Essex. A nursery-cry.—It is also sometimes sung in the streets by boys who have small figures of
wool, wood, or gypsum, &c., of lambs to sell.

Young lambs to sell!
Young lambs to sell!
If I'd as much money as I can tell,
I never would cry—Young lambs to sell!

401

From Yorkshire. A nursery-cry.

Rabbit, rabbit, rabbit-pie!
Come, my ladies, come and buy;
Else your babies they will cry.

402

To market, to market,
To buy a plum cake;
Home again, home again,
Ne'er a one baked;
The baker is dead and all his men,
And we must go to market again.

403

Rock well my cradle,
And "bee baa", my son;
You shall have a new gown,
When ye lord comes home.

Oh! still my child, Orange,
Still him with a bell;
I can't still him, ladie,
Till you come down yoursell.

404

Where was a sugar and fretty?
  And where was jewel and spicy?
Hush-a-bye babe in a cradle,
  And we'll go away in a tricy?

405

I'll buy you a tartan bonnet,
And some feathers to put on it,
Tartan trews and a philibeg,
Because you are like your daddy.

Jingles

406

The first line of the following is the burden of a song in the
"Tempest", act i. sc. 2, and also of one in the "Merchant of
Venice", act iii, sc. 2.

> Ding, dong, bell,
> Pussy's in the well!
> Who put her in?—
> Little Tommy Lin.
> Who pulled her out?—
> Dog with long snout.
> What a naughty boy was that
> To drown poor pussy-cat,
> Who never did any harm,
> But kill'd the mice in his father's barn.

407

> Hey ding a ding, what shall I sing?
> How many holes in a skimmer?

Four and twenty,—my stomach is empty;
Pray, mamma, give me some dinner.

408

Cock a doodle doo!
My dame has lost her shoe;
My master's lost his fiddling stick,
And don't know what to do.

Cock a doodle doo!
What is my dame to do?
Till master finds his fiddling stick
She'll dance without her shoe.

Cock a doodle doo!
My dame has lost her shoe,
And master's found his fiddling stick,
Sing doodle doodle doo!

Cock a doodle doo!
My dame will dance with you,
While master fiddles his fiddling stick,
For dame and doodle doo.

Cock a doodle doo!
Dame has lost her shoe;
Gone to bed and scratch'd her head,
And can't tell what to do.

409

Diddledy, diddledy, dumpty;
The cat ran up the plum-tree.
I'll lay you a crown
I'll fetch you down;
So diddledy, diddledy, dumpty.

410

Little Tee Wee,
He went to sea
In an open boat:
And while afloat
The little boat bended,
And my story's ended.

411

Sing, sing, what shall I sing?
The cat has ate the pudding-string!
Do, do, what shall I do?
The cat has bit it quite in two.

412

I do not know whether the following may have reference to the
game of handy-dandy, mentioned in "King Lear", act iv. sc. 6,
and in Florio's "New World of Words", 1611, p. 57.

Handy Spandy, Jack-a-dandy
Loved plum-cake and sugar-candy;
He bought some at a grocer's shop,
And out he came, hop, hop, hop.

413

Tiddle liddle lightum,
Pitch and tar;
Tiddle liddle lightum,
What's that for?

414

Sing jigmijole, the pudding-bowl,
The table and the frame;
My master he did cudgel me
For speaking of my dame.

415

Deedle, deedle, dumpling, my son John
Went to bed with his trousers on;
One shoe off, the other shoe on,
Deedle, deedle, dumpling, my son John.

416

Dibbity, dibbity, dibbity, doe,
Give me a pancake
  And I'll go.
Dibbity, dibbity, dibbity, ditter,
Please to give me
  A bit of a fritter.

417

Feedum, fiddledum, fee,
The cat's got into the tree.
  Pussy, come down,
  Or I'll crack your crown,
And toss you into the sea.

418

Little Jack a Dandy
Wanted sugar-candy,
And fairly for it cried;
  But Little Billy Cook
  Who always reads his book,
Shall have a horse to ride.

419

Hyder iddle diddle dell,
A yard of pudding's not an ell;
Not forgetting tweedle-dye,
A tailor's goose will never fly.

420

Gilly Silly Jarter,
Who has lost a garter?
In a shower of rain,
The miller found it,
The miller ground it,
And the miller gave it to Silly again.

421

Hub a dub dub,
Three men in a tub;
And who do you think they be?
The butcher, the baker,
The candlestick-maker;
Turn 'em out knaves all three!

422

Hey diddle dinketty, poppety, pet,
The merchants of London they wear scarlet;
Silk in the collar, and gold in the hem,
So merrily march the merchantmen.

423

Fiddle-de-dee, fiddle-de-dee,
The fly shall marry the humble-bee.
They went to the church, and married was she;
The fly has married the humble-bee.

424

Hey, dorolot, dorolot!
Hey, dorolay, dorolay!
Hey, my bonny boat, bonny boat,
Hey, drag away, drag away!

425

A cat came fiddling out of a barn,
With a pair of bagpipes under her arm;
She could sing nothing but fiddle cum fee,
The mouse has married the humble-bee.
Pipe, cat,—dance, mouse,
We'll have a wedding at our good house.

426

Hey! diddle, diddle,
The cat and the fiddle,
The cow jumped over the moon;
The little dog laugh'd
To see the sport,
While the dish ran after the spoon.

427

Doodledy, doodledy, doodledy, dan,
I'll have a piper to be my good man;
And if I get less meat, I shall get game,
Doodledy, doodledy, doodledy, dan.

428

Tweedle-dum and tweedle-dee
Resolved to have a battle,
For tweedle-dum said tweedle-dee
Had spoiled his nice new rattle.
Just then flew by a monstrous crow,
As big as a tar-barrel,
Which frightened both the heroes so,
They quite forgot their quarrel.

429

Come dance a jig
To my granny's pig,
With a raudy, rowdy, dowdy;
Come dance a jig
To my granny's pig,
And pussy-cat shall crowdy.

430

Pussicat, wussicat, with a white foot,
When is your wedding? for I'll come to't.
The beer's to brew, the bread's to bake,
Pussy-cat, pussy-cat, don't be too late.

431

Ding, dong, darrow,
The cat and the sparrow;
The little dog has burnt his tail,
And he shall be hang'd to-morrow.

432

Little Dicky Dilver
Had a wife of silver,
He took a stick and broke her back,
And sold her to the miller;
The miller wouldn't have her,
So he threw her in the river.

433

To market, to market, to buy a fat pig,
Home again, home again, dancing a jig;
Ride to the market to buy a fat hog,
Home again, home again, jiggety-jog.

434

Doodle, doodle, doo,
The princess lost her shoe;
Her highness hopp'd,
The fiddler stopp'd,
Not knowing what to do.

435

Rompty-iddity, row, row, row;
If I had a good supper, I could eat it now.

436

Magotty-pie is given in MS. Lands. 1033, fol. 2, as a Wiltshire
word for a magpie. See also "Macbeth", act iii. sc. 4. The same
term occurs in the dictionaries of Hollyband, Cotgrave, and
Minsheu.

Round about, round about,
Magotty-pie;
My father loves good ale,
And so do I.

437

High, ding, cockatoo-moody,
Make a bed in a barn, I will come to thee;
High, ding, straps of leather,
Two little puppy-dogs tied together;
One by the head, and one by the tail,
And over the water these puppy-dogs sail.

438

Our collection of nursery songs may appropriately be con-
cluded with the Quaker's commentary on one of the greatest
favourites—Hey! diddle, diddle. We have endeavoured, as far
as practicable, to remove every line from the present edition
that could offend the most fastidious ear; but the following

annotations on a song we cannot be induced to omit, would appear to suggest that our endeavours are scarcely likely to be attended with success.

"Hey! diddle, diddle,
The cat and the fiddle"—

Yes, thee may say that, for that is nonsense.

"The cow jumped over the moon"—

Oh, no! Mary, thee mustn't say that, for that is a falsehood; thee knows a cow could never jump over the moon; but a cow may jump under it: so thee ought to say—"The cow jumped *under* the moon." Yes,—

"The cow jumped under the moon;
The little dog laughed"—

Oh, Mary, stop. How can a little dog laugh? thee knows a little dog can't laugh. Thee ought to say—"The little dog *barked* to see the sport."

"And the dish ran after the spoon"—

Stop, Mary, stop. A dish could never run after a spoon; thee ought to know that. Thee had better say—"And the *cat* ran after the spoon." So,—

"Hey! diddle, diddle,
  The cat and the fiddle,
The cow jumped *under* the moon;
  The little dog *barked*,
  To see the sport,
And the *cat* ran after the spoon!"

Love and Matrimony

439

As I was going up Pippen-hill,
    Pippen-hill was dirty,
There I met a pretty miss,
    And she dropt me a curtsey.

Little miss, pretty miss,
    Blessings light upon you!
If I had half-a-crown a day,
    I'd spend it all on you.

440

Brave news is come to town,
    Brave news is carried;
Brave news is come to town,
    Jemmy Dawson's married.

441

Willy, Willy, Wilkin,
Kissed the maids a-milkin',
            Fa, la, la!

175

And with his merry daffing,
He set them all a laughing,
              Ha, ha, ha!

442

It's once I courted as pretty a lass
   As ever your eyes did see;
But now she's come to such a pass,
   She never will do for me.

She invited me to her own house,
   Where oft I'd been before,
And she tumbled me into the hog-tub;
   I'll never go there any more.

443

Sylvia, sweet as morning air,
Do not drive me to despair:
Long have I sighed in vain,
Now I am come again.
   Will you be mine or no, no-a-no,—
   Will you be mine or no?

Simon, pray leave off your suit,
For of your courting you'll reap no fruit;
I would rather give a crown
Than be married to a clown;
   Go, for a booby, go, no-a-no,—
   Go, for a booby, go.

444

What care I how black I be,
Twenty pounds will marry me;
If twenty won't, forty shall,
I am my mother's bouncing girl!

445

"Where have you been all the day,
    My boy Willy?"

"I've been all the day
Courting of a lady gay:
But oh! she's too young
To be taken from her mammy."

"What work can she do,
    My boy Willy?
Can she bake and can she brew,
    My boy Willy?"

"She can brew and she can bake,
And she can make our wedding cake:
But oh! she's too young
To be taken from her mammy."

"What age may she be? What age may she be?
    My boy Willy?"

"Twice two, twice seven,
Twice ten, twice eleven:
But oh! she's too young
To be taken from her mammy."

446

This is part of a little work called "Authentic Memoirs of the little Man and the little Maid, with some interesting particulars of their lives", which I suspect is more modern than the following. Walpole printed a small broadside containing a different version.

There was a little man,
  And he woo'd a little maid,
And he said, "Little maid, will you wed, wed, wed?
  I have little more to say,
  Than will you, yea or nay,
For least said is soonest mended-ded, ded, ded."

The little maid replied,
Some say a little sighed,
"But what shall we have for to eat, eat, eat?
Will the love that you're so rich in
Make a fire in the kitchen?
Or the little god of Love turn the spit, spit, spit?"

447

There was a little boy and a little girl
  Lived in an alley;
Says the little boy to the little girl,
  "Shall I, oh! shall I?"

Says the little girl to the little boy,
  "What shall we do?"
Says the little boy to the little girl,
  "I will kiss you."

448

A cow and a calf,
  An ox and a half,
Forty good shillings and three;
  Is that not enough tocher
  For a shoemaker's daughter,
A bonny lass with a black e'e?

449

O the little rusty, dusty, rusty miller!
I'll not change my wife for either gold or siller.

450

As Tommy Snooks and Bessy Brooks
  Were walking out one Sunday,
Says Tommy Snooks to Bessy Brooks,
  "To-morrow will be Monday."

451

Little Jack Jingle,
He used to live single:
But when he got tired of this kind of life,
He left off being single, and lived with his wife.

452

When shall we be married,
  My dear Nicholas Wood?
We will be married on Monday,
  And will not that be very good?
What, shall we be married no sooner?
  Why sure the man's gone wood!*

What shall we have for our dinner,
  My dear Nicholas Wood?
We will have bacon and pudding,
  And will not that be very good?
What, shall we have nothing more?
  Why sure the man's gone wood!

Who shall we have at our wedding,
  My dear Nicholas Wood?
We will have mammy and daddy,
  And will not that be very good?
What, shall we have nobody else?
  Why sure the man's gone wood!

*Mad. This sense of the word has long been obsolete; and
exhibits, therefore, the antiquity of these lines.

453

Tommy Trot, a man of law,
Sold his bed and lay upon straw:
Sold the straw and slept on grass,
To buy his wife a looking-glass.

179

454

We're all dry with drinking on't;
We're all dry with drinking on't;
The piper spoke to the fiddler's wife,
And I can't sleep for thinking on't.

455

"John, come sell thy fiddle,
  And buy thy wife a gown."
"No, I'll not sell my fiddle,
  For ne'er a wife in town."

456

Up hill and down dale;
Butter is made in every vale;
And if that Nancy Cook
Is a good girl,
She shall have a spouse,
And make butter anon,
Before her old grandmother
Grows a young man.

457

Jack in the pulpit, out and in;
Sold his wife for a minikin pin.

458

Did you see my wife, did you see, did you see,
  Did you see my wife looking for me?
She wears a straw bonnet, with white ribbons on it,
  And dimity petticoats over her knee.

459

Rosemary green,
And lavender blue,
Thyme and sweet marjorum,
Hyssop and rue.

460

"Little maid, pretty maid, whither goest thou?"
"Down in the forest to milk my cow."
"Shall I go with thee?" "No not now;
When I send for thee, then come thou."

461

I am a pretty wench,
And I come a great way hence,
And sweethearts I can get none:
But every dirty sow,
Can get sweethearts enow,
And I, pretty wench, can get never a one.

462

Birds of a feather flock together,
And so will pigs and swine;
Rats and mice will have their choice,
And so will I have mine.

463

The practice of sowing hempseed on Allhallows Even is often
alluded to by earlier writers, and Gay, in his "Pastorals",
quotes part of the following lines as used on that occasion.

Hempseed I set,
Hempseed I sow,
The young man that I love,
Come after me and mow!

464

Jack Sprat could eat no fat,
 His wife could eat no lean;
And so, betwixt them both, you see,
 They lick'd the platter clean.

465

Little Jack Dandy-prat was my first suitor;
He had a dish and a spoon, and he'd some pewter;
He'd linen and woollen, and woollen and linen,
A little pig in a string cost him five shilling.

466

THE KEYS OF CANTERBURY

Oh, madam, I will give you the keys of Canterbury,
To set all the bells ringing when we shall be merry,
If you will but walk abroad with me,
If you will but talk with me.

Sir, I'll not accept of the keys of Canterbury,
To set all the bells ringing when we shall be merry:
Neither will I walk abroad with thee,
Neither will I talk with thee!

Oh, madam, I will give you a fine carved comb,
To comb out your ringlets when I am from home,
If you will but walk with me, &c.
 Sir, I'll not accept, &c.

Oh, madam, I will give you a pair of shoes of cork,*
One made in London, the other made in York,
If you will but walk with me, &c.
 Sir, I'll not accept, &c.

 * This proves the song was not later than the era of chopines, or
high cork shoes.

Madam, I will give you a sweet silver bell,*
To ring up your maidens when you are not well,
If you will but walk with me, &c.
   Sir, I'll not accept, &c.

Oh, my man John, what can the matter be?
I love the lady and the lady loves not me!
Neither will she walk abroad with me,
Neither will she talk with me.

Oh, master dear, do not despair,
The lady she shall be, shall be your only dear,
And she will walk and talk with thee,
And she will walk with thee!

Oh, madam, I will give you the keys of my chest,
To count my gold and silver when I am gone to rest,
If you will but walk abroad with me,
If you will but talk with me.

Oh, sir, I will accept of the keys of your chest,
To count your gold and silver when you are gone to rest,
And I will walk abroad with thee,
And I will talk with thee!

     * Another proof of antiquity. It must probably have been
written before the invention of bell-pulls.

467

He. If you with me will go, my love,
    You shall see a pretty show, my love,
      Let dame say what she will:
    If you will have me, my love,
    I will have thee, my love,
      So let the milk-pail stand still.

She. Since you have said so, my love,
    Longer I will go, my love,
      Let dame say what she will:

If you will have me, my love,
I will have thee, my love,
    So let the milk-pail stand still.

468

On Saturday night
Shall be all my care,
To powder my locks
And curl my hair.

On Sunday morning
My love will come in,
When he will marry me
With a gold ring.

469

Master I have, and I am his man,
    Gallop a dreary dun;
Master I have, and I am his man,
And I'll get a wife as fast as I can;
With a heighly gaily gamberaily,
    Higgledy piggledy, niggledy, niggledy,
    Gallop a dreary dun.

470

I doubt, I doubt, my fire is out,
    My little wife isn't at home;
I'll saddle my dog, and I'll bridle my cat,
    And I'll go fetch my little wife home.

471

Young Roger came tapping at Dolly's window,
Thumpaty, thumpaty, thump!
He asked for admittance, she answered him "No!"
Frumpaty, frumpaty, frump!

"No, no, Roger, no! as you came you may go!"
Stumpaty, stumpaty, stump!

472

Thomas and Annis met in the dark.
  "Good morning," said Thomas.
  "Good morning," said Annis.
And so they began to talk.

"I'll give you," says Thomas.
"Give me," said Annis;
  "I prithee, love, tell me what?"
"Some nuts," said Thomas.
"Some nuts," said Annis;
  "Nuts are good to crack."

"I love you," said Thomas.
"Love me!" said Annis;
  "I prithee, love, tell me where?"
"In my heart," said Thomas.
"In your heart!" said Annis;
  "How came you to love me there?"

"I'll marry you," said Thomas.
"Marry me!" said Annis;
  "I prithee, love, tell me when?"
"Next Sunday," said Thomas.
"Next Sunday," said Annis;
  "I wish next Sunday were come."

473

Saw ye aught of my love a coming from ye market?
  A pack of meal upon her back,
  A baby in her basket;
Saw ye aught of my love a coming from ye market?

474

This nursery song may probably commemorate a part of Tom Thumb's history, extant in a little Danish work, treating of "Swain Tomling, a man no bigger than a thumb, who would be married to a woman three ells and three quarters long". See Mr Thoms' Preface to "Tom à Lincoln", p. xi.

> I had a little husband,
>   No bigger than my thumb;
> I put him in a pint pot,
>   And there I bid him drum.
>
> I bought a little horse,
>   That galloped up and down;
> I bridled him, and saddled him,
>   And sent him out of town.
>
> I gave him some garters,
>   To garter up his hose,
> And a little handkerchief,
>   To wipe his pretty nose.

475

> Can you make me a cambric shirt,
>   Parsley, sage, rosemary, and thyme;
> Without any seam or needle-work?
>   And you shall be a true lover of mine.
>
> Can you wash it in yonder well,
>   Parsley, &c.
> Where never sprung water, nor rain ever fell?
>   And you, &c.
>
> Can you dry it on yonder thorn,
>   Parsley, &c.
> Which never bore blossom since Adam was born?
>   And you, &c.

Now you have asked me questions three,
   Parsley, &c.
I hope you'll answer as many for me,
   And you, &c.

Can you find me an acre of land,
   Parsley, &c.
Between the salt water and the sea sand?
   And you, &c.

Can you plough it with a ram's horn,
   Parsley, &c.
And sow it all over with one pepper-corn?
   And you, &c.

Can you reap it with a sickle of leather,
   Parsley, &c.
And bind it up with a peacock's feather?
   And you, &c.

When you have done and finish'd your work,
   Parsley, &c.
Then come to me for your cambric shirt,
   And you, &c.

476

Where have you been to-day, Billy, my son?
Where have you been to-day, my only man?
I've been a-wooing, mother; make my bed soon,
For I'm sick at heart, and fain would lie down.

What have you ate to-day, Billy, my son?
What have you ate to-day, my only man?
I've ate an eel-pie, mother; make my bed soon,
For I'm sick at heart, and shall die before noon!

477

I married my wife by the light of the moon,
   A tidy housewife, a tidy one;
She never gets up until it is noon,
   And I hope she'll prove a tidy one.

And when she gets up, she is slovenly laced,
   A tidy, &c.
She takes up the poker to roll out the paste,
   And I hope, &c.

She churns her butter in a boot,
   A tidy, &c.
And instead of a churnstaff she puts in her foot,
   And I hope, &c.

She lays her cheese on the scullery shelf,
   A tidy, &c.
And she never turns it till it turns itself,
   And I hope, &c.

478

There was a little maid, and she was afraid,
That her sweetheart would come unto her;
So she went to bed, and cover'd up her head,
And fasten'd the door with a skewer.

479

"Madam, I am come to court you,
If your favour I can gain."
"Ah, ah!" said she, "you are a bold fellow,
If I e'er see your face again!"

"Madam, I have rings and diamonds,
Madam, I have houses and land,
Madam, I have a world of treasure,
All shall be at your command."

"I care not for rings and diamonds,
I care not for houses and lands,
I care not for a world of treasure,
So that I have but a handsome man."

"Madam, you think much of beauty,
Beauty hasteneth to decay,
For the fairest of flowers that grow in summer,
Will decay and fade away."

480

Up street, and down street,
   Each window's made of glass;
If you go to Tommy Tickler's house,
   You'll find a pretty lass.

481

Oh! mother, I shall be married to Mr Punchinello.
  To Mr Punch,
  To Mr Joe,
  To Mr Nell,
  To Mr Lo,
  Mr Punch, Mr Joe,
  Mr Nell, Mr Lo,
  To Mr Punchinello.

482

Little John Jiggy Jag,
  He rode a penny nag,
And went to Wigan to woo:
  When he came to a beck,
  He fell and broke his neck,—
Johnny, how dost thou now?

I made him a hat,
Of my coat-lap,
And stockings of pearly blue:
A hat and a feather,
To keep out cold weather;
So, Johnny, how dost thou now?

483

Cumberland courtship.

Bonny lass, canny lass, willta be mine?
Thou'se neither wesh dishes, nor sarrah (*serve*) the swine;
Thou sall sit on a cushion, and sew up a seam,
And thou sall eat strawberries, sugar, and cream!

484

Bessy Bell and Mary Gray,*
They were two bonny lasses:
They built their house upon the lea,
And covered it with rashes.

Bessy kept the garden gate,
And Mary kept the pantry:
Bessy always had to wait,
While Mary lived in plenty.

* The common tradition respecting these celebrated beauties
is as follows: "In the year 1666, when the plague raged at Perth,
these ladies retired into solitude, to avoid infection; built on a
small streamlet, tributary to the Almond, in a sequestered corner
called *Burn-brae*, a bower, and lived in it together, till a young
man, whom they both tenderly loved, in his visits communicated
to them the fatal contagion, of which they soon after died."

485

Jack and Jill went up the hill,
To fetch a pail of water;
Jack fell down and broke his crown,
And Jill came tumbling after.

486

Little Tom Dandy
    Was my first suitor,
He had a spoon and dish,
    And a little pewter.

487

There was a little pretty lad,
    And he lived by himself,
And all the meat he got
    He put upon a shelf.

The rats and the mice
    Did lead him such a life,
That he went to Ireland
    To get himself a wife.

The lanes they were so broad,
    And the fields they were so narrow,
He couldn't get his wife home
    Without a wheelbarrow.

The wheelbarrow broke,
    My wife she got a kick,
The deuce take the wheelbarrow,
    That spared my wife's neck.

488

Rowley Poley, pudding and pie,
Kissed the girls and made them cry;
When the girls begin to cry,
Rowley Poley runs away.

489

Margaret wrote a letter,
    Seal'd it with her finger,

Threw it in the dam
For the dusty miller.
Dusty was his coat,
Dusty was the siller,
Dusty was the kiss
I'd from the dusty miller.
If I had my pockets
Full of gold and siller,
I would give it all
To my dusty miller.

Chorus
O the little, little,
Rusty, dusty, miller.

490

Love your own, kiss your own.
  Love your own mother, hinny;
For if she was dead and gone,
  You'd ne'er get such another, hinny.

491

Here comes a lusty wooer,
  My a dildin, my a daldin;
Here comes a lusty wooer,
  Lily bright and shine a'.

Pray, who do you woo,
  My a dildin, my a daldin?
Pray, who do you woo,
  Lily bright and shine a'?

For your fairest daughter,
  My a dildin, my a daldin;
For your fairest daughter,
  Lily bright and shine a'.

Then there she is for you,
   My a dildin, my a daldin;
Then there she is for you,
   Lily bright and shine a'.

492

O rare Harry Parry,
   When will you marry?
When apples and pears are ripe.
   I'll come to your wedding,
   Without any bidding,
And dance and sing all the night.

493

Blue eye beauty,
Grey eye greedy,
Black eye blackie,
Brown eye brownie.

494

Curly locks, curly locks! wilt thou be mine?
Thou shalt not wash dishes, nor yet feed the swine;

But sit on a cushion and sew a fine seam,
And feed upon strawberries, sugar, and cream!

Natural History

495

The cuckoo's a fine bird,
   He sings as he flies;
He brings us good tidings,
   He tells us no lies.

He sucks little birds' eggs,
   To make his voice clear;
And when he sings "cuckoo!"
   The summer is near.

496

A provincial version of the same.

The cuckoo's a vine bird,
   A zengs as a vlies;
A brengs us good tidin's,
   And tells us no lies.

A zucks th' smael birds' eggs,
   To make his voice clear;
And the mwore a cries "cuckoo!"
   The zummer draws near.

497

I had a little dog, and his name was Blue Bell,
I gave him some work, and he did it very well;
I sent him up stairs to pick up a pin,
He stepped in the coal-scuttle up to the chin;
I sent him to the garden to pick some sage,
He tumbled down and fell in a rage;
I sent him to the cellar to draw a pot of beer,
He came up again and said there was none there.

498

The cat sat asleep by the side of the fire,
    The mistress snored loud as a pig:
Jack took up his fiddle, by Jenny's desire,
    And struck up a bit of a jig.

499

I had a little hobby-horse, and it was well shod,
It carried me to the mill door, trod, trod, trod;
When I got there I gave a great shout,
Down came the hobby-horse, and I cried out.
Fie upon the miller, he was a great beast,
He would not come to my house, I made a little feast,
I had but little, but I would give him some,
For playing of his bagpipes and beating of his drum.

500

    Pit, pat, well-a-day,
    Little Robin flew away;
    Where can little Robin be?
    Gone into the cherry-tree.

501

Little Poll Parrot
Sat in his garret,
   Eating toast and tea;
A little brown mouse,
Jumped into the house,
   And stole it all away.

502

The snail scoops out hollows, little rotund chambers, in lime-
stone, for its residence. This habit of the animal is so important
in its effects, as to have attracted the attention of geologists, and
Dr Buckland alluded to it at the meeting of the British Associa-
tion in 1841. See Chambers' "Popular Rhymes", p. 43. The
following rhyme is a boy's invocation to the snail to come out of
such holes.

Snail, snail, come out of your hole,
Or else I will beat you as black as a coal.

503

  Sneel, snaul,
Robbers are coming to pull down your wall;
  Sneel, snaul,
  Put out your horn,
Robbers are coming to steal your corn,
Coming at four o'clock in the morn.

504

Burnie bee, burnie bee,
Tell me when your wedding be?
If it be to-morrow day,
Take your wings and fly away.

505

Some little mice sat in a barn to spin;
Pussy came by, and popped her head in;
"Shall I come in, and cut your threads off?"
"Oh! no, kind sir, you will snap our heads off."

506

The sow came in with the saddle,
The little pig rock'd the cradle,
The dish jump'd over the table,
To see the pot with the ladle.
The broom behind the butt
Call'd the dish-clout a nasty slut:
"Oh! oh!" says the gridiron, "can't you agree?
I'm the head constable,—come along with me."

507

"What do they call you?"
"Patchy Dolly."
"Where were you born?"
"In the cow's horn."
"Where were you bred?"
"In the cow's head."
"Where will you die?"
"In the cow's eye."

508

As I went over the water,
The water went over me.
I saw two little blackbirds sitting on a tree:
The one called me a rascal,
The other called me a thief;
I took up my little black stick,
And knocked out all their teeth.

509

Four and twenty tailors went to kill a snail,
The best man among them durst not touch her tail;
She put out her horns like a little Kyloe cow,
Run, tailors, run, or she'll kill you all e'en now.

510

A Dorsetshire version.

'Twas the twenty-ninth of May, 'twas a holiday,
Four and twenty tailors set out to hunt a snail;
The snail put forth her horns, and roared like a bull,
Away ran the tailors, and catch the snail who wull.

511

Croak! said the Toad, I'm hungry, I think,
To-day I've had nothing to eat or to drink,
I'll crawl to a garden and jump through the pales,
And there I'll dine nicely on slugs and on snails;
Ho, ho! quoth the Frog, is that what you mean?
Then I'll hop away to the next meadow stream,
There I will drink, and eat worms and slugs too,
And then I shall have a good dinner like you.

512

Gray goose and gander,
    Waft your wings together,
And carry the good king's daughter
    Over the one strand river.

513

Pussy-cat, pussy-cat, where have you been?
I've been up to London to look at the queen.
Pussy-cat, pussy-cat, what did you there?
I frighten'd a little mouse under the chair.

514

I had a little dog, and they call'd him Buff;
I sent him to the shop for a hap'orth of snuff;
But he lost the bag, and spill'd the snuff,
So take that cuff, and that's enough.

515

All of a row,
Bend the bow,
Shot at a pigeon,
And killed a crow.

516

The cock doth crow
To let you know,
If you be wise,
'Tis time to rise.

517

There was an owl lived in an oak,
  Wisky, wasky, weedle;
And every word he ever spoke
  Was fiddle, faddle, feedle.

A gunner chanced to come that way,
  Wisky, wasky, weedle;
Says he, "I'll shoot you, silly bird."
  Fiddle, faddle, feedle.

518

When the snow is on the ground
  Little Robin Red-breast grieves;
For no berries can be found,
  And on the trees there are no leaves.

The air is cold, the worms are hid,
  For this poor bird what can be done?
We'll strew him here some crumbs of bread,
  And then he'll live till the snow is gone.

519

A pie sate on a pear-tree,
A pie sate on a pear-tree,
A pie sate on a pear-tree,
  Heigh O, heigh O, heigh O!
Once so merrily hopp'd she,
Twice so merrily hopp'd she,
Thrice so merrily hopp'd she,
  Heigh O, heigh O, heigh O!

520

An ancient Suffolk song for a bad singer.

There was an old crow
  Sat upon a clod:
There's an end of my song,
  That's odd!

521

Cuckoo, Cuckoo,
What do you do?
In April
I open my bill;
In May
I sing night and day;
In June
I change my tune;
In July
Away I fly;
In August
Away I must.

522

"Robert Barnes, fellow fine,
Can you shoe this horse of mine?"
"Yes, good sir, that I can,
As well as any other man;
There's a nail, and there's a prod,
And now, good sir, your horse is shod."

523

Catch him, crow! carry him, kite!
Take him away till the apples are ripe!
When they are ripe and ready to fall,
Home comes [Johnny], apples and all.

524

Dickery, dickery, dare,
The pig flew up in the air;
The man in brown soon brought him down,
Dickery, dickery, dare.

525

Hickety, pickety, my black hen,
She lays eggs for gentlemen;
Gentlemen come every day
To see what my black hen doth lay.

526

Pussy sat by the fire-side
In a basket full of coal-dust;
Bas-
ket,
Coal-
dust,
In a basket full of coal-dust!

527

Little Robin Red-breast
　Sat upon a rail:
Niddle naddle went his head,
　Wiggle waggle went his tail.

528

Little Robin Red-breast
　Sat upon a hirdle;
With a pair of speckled legs,
　And a green girdle.

529

Johnny Armstrong kill'd a calf,
Peter Henderson got the half;
Willy Wilkinson got the head.
Ring the bell, the calf is dead!

530

Hie hie, says Anthony,
Puss in the pantry
Gnawing, gnawing
A mutton mutton-bone;
See now she tumbles it,
See now she mumbles it,
See how she tosses
The mutton mutton-bone.

531

A long-tail'd pig, or a short-tail'd pig,
Or a pig without e'er a tail,
A sow-pig, or a boar-pig,
Or a pig with a curly tail.

532

Once I saw a little bird
Come hop, hop, hop;
So I cried, little bird,
Will you stop, stop, stop?
And was going to the window
To say How do you do?
But he shook his little tail,
And far away he flew.

533

The following stanza is of very considerable antiquity, and is
common in Yorkshire. See Hunter's "Hallamshire Glossary",
p. 56.

Lady-cow, lady-cow, fly thy way home,
Thy house is on fire, thy children all gone,
All but one that ligs under a stone,
Fly thee home, lady-cow, ere it be gone.

534

Riddle me, riddle me, ree,
A hawk sate up on a tree;
And he says to himself, says he,
Oh dear! what a fine bird I be!

535

Bird boy's song.

Eat, birds, eat, and make no waste,
I lie here and make no haste;
If my master chance to come,
You must fly, and I must run.

536

Pussy-cat Mole,
Jump'd over a coal,

And in her best petticoat burnt a great hole.
Poor pussy's weeping, she'll have no more milk,
Until her best petticoat's mended with silk.

537

As I went to Bonner,
  I met a pig
  Without a wig,
Upon my word and honour.

538

There was a little one-eyed gunner
Who kill'd all the birds that died last summer.

539

There was a piper, he'd a cow;
  And he'd no hay to give her;
He took his pipes and played a tune,
  Consider, old cow, consider!

The cow considered very well,
  For she gave the piper a penny,
That he might play the tune again,
  Of corn rigs are bonnie!

540

As titty mouse sat in the witty to spin,
Pussy came to her and bid her good ev'n.
"Oh, what are you doing, my little oman?"
"A spinning a doublet for my gude man."
"Then shall I come to thee and wind up thy thread!"
"Oh no, Mrs Puss, you'll bite off my head."

541

Shoe the colt,
Shoe the colt,
Shoe the wild mare;
Here a nail,
There a nail,
Yet she goes bare.

542

Betty Pringle had a little pig,
Not very little and not very big,
When he was alive he lived in clover,
But now he's dead, and that's all over.
So Billy Pringle he lay down and cried,
And Betty Pringle she lay down and died;
So there was an end of one, two, and three;
    Billy Pringle he,
    Betty Pringle she,
    And the piggy wiggy.

543

Cock Robin got up early,
    At the break of day,
And went to Jenny's window
    To sing a roundelay.

He sang Cock Robin's love
    To the pretty Jenny Wren,
And when he got unto the end,
    Then he began again.

544

I had two pigeons bright and gay,
They flew from me the other day;

What was the reason they did go?
I cannot tell, for I do not know.

545

Jack Sprat's pig,
He was not very little,
Nor yet very big;
He was not very lean,
He was not very fat;
He'll do well for a grunt,
Says little Jack Sprat.

546

The proverb of Barnaby Bright is given by Ray and Brand as referring to St Barnabas.

Barnaby Bright he was a sharp cur,
He always would bark if a mouse did but stir;
But now he's grown old, and can no longer bark,
He's condemn'd by the parson to be hang'd by the clerk.

547

Pussy-cat ate the dumplings, the dumplings,
Pussy-cat ate the dumplings.
    Mamma stood by,
    And cried, Oh, fie!
Why did you eat the dumplings?

548

The robin and the wren,
They fought upon the parrage pan;
But ere the robin got a spoon,
The wren had ate the parrage down.

549

Little Bob Robin,
Where do you live?
Up in yonder wood, sir,
On a hazel twig.

550

The winds they did blow,
   The leaves they did wag;
Along came a beggar boy,
   And put me in his bag.

He took me up to London,
   A lady did me buy,
Put me in a silver cage,
   And hung me up on high.

With apples by the fire,
   And nuts for to crack,
Besides a little feather bed
   To rest my little back.

551

I had a little cow, to save her,
I turned her into the meadow to graze her;
There came a heavy storm of rain,
And drove the little cow home again.
The church doors they stood open,
And there the little cow was cropen:
The bell-ropes they were made of hay,
And the little cow ate them all away:
The sexton came to toll the bell,
And pushed the little cow into the well!

552

In the month of February,
  When green leaves begin to spring,
Little lambs do skip like fairies,
  Birds do ouple, build, and sing.

553

Pussy sits behind the fire,
  How can she be fair?
In comes the little dog,
  Pussy, are you there?
So, so, Mistress Pussy,
  Pray how do you do?
Thank you, thank you, little dog,
  I'm very well just now.

554

The dove says coo, coo, what shall I do?
I can scarce maintain two.
Pooh, pooh, says the wren, I have got ten,
And keep them all like gentlemen!

555

Bow, wow, wow,
  Whose dog art thou?
Little Tom Tinker's dog,
  Bow, wow, wow.

556

Pitty Patty Polt,
Shoe the wild colt!

Here a nail,
And there a nail,
Pitty Patty Polt.

557

How d' 'e dogs, how? whose dog art thou?
Little Tom Tinker's dog! what's that to thou?
Hiss! bow a wow, wow!

558

Robbin-a-Bobbin bent his bow,
And shot at a woodcock and kill'd a yowe:
The yowe cried ba, and he ran away,
But never came back 'till midsummer-day.

559

A little cock-sparrow sat on a green tree, (*tris*)
And he cherruped, he cherruped, so merry was he; (*tris*)
A little cock-sparrow sat on a green tree,
And he cherruped, he cherruped, so merry was he.

A naughty boy came with his wee bow and arrow, (*tris*)
Determined to shoot this little cock-sparrow, (*tris*)
A naughty, &c.
Determined, &c.

This little cock-sparrow shall make me a stew, (*tris*)
And his giblets shall make a little pie too, (*tris*)
Oh, no! said ye sparrow, I *won't* make a stew,
So he flapped his wings and away he flew!

560

Snail, snail, put out your horns,
I'll give you bread and barley-corns.

561

The following song is given in Whiter's "Specimen, or a Commentary on Shakespeare", 8vo. London, 1794, p. 19, as common in Cambridgeshire and Norfolk. Dr Farmer gives another version as an illustration of a ditty of Jacques in "As You Like It", act. ii. sc. 5. See Malone's Shakespeare, ed. 1821, vol. vi. p. 398; Caldecott's "Specimen", 1819, note on "As You Like It", p. 11; and Douce's "Illustrations", vol. i. p. 297.

Dame, what makes your ducks to die?
What the pize ails 'em? what the pize ails 'em?
They kick up their heels, and there they lie,
What the pize ails 'em now?
  Heigh, ho! heigh, ho!

Dame, what makes your ducks to die?
What a pize ails 'em? what a pize ails 'em?
  Heigh, ho! heigh, ho!

Dame, what ails your ducks to die?
Eating o' polly-wigs, eating o' polly-wigs.
  Heigh, ho! heigh, ho!

562

Lady bird, lady bird, fly away home,
Thy house is on fire, thy children all gone,
All but one, and her name is Ann,
And she crept under the pudding-pan.

563

Little Robin Red-breast sat upon a tree,
Up went Pussy-cat, and down went he;
Down came Pussy-cat, and away Robin ran;
Says little Robin Red-breast, "Catch me if you can."

Little Robin Red-breast jump'd upon a wall,
Pussy-cat jump'd after him, and almost got a fall;

Little Robin chirp'd and sang, and what did Pussy say?
Pussy-cat said "Mew," and Robin jump'd away.

564

There was a little boy went into a barn,
 And lay down on some hay;
An owl came out and flew about,
 And the little boy ran away.

565

Snail, snail, shut out your horns;
 Father and mother are dead:
Brother and sister are in the back yard,
 Begging for barley bread.

566

I had a little hen, the prettiest ever seen,
She washed me the dishes, and kept the house clean:
She went to the mill to fetch me some flour,
She brought it home in less than an hour;
She baked me my bread, she brew'd me my ale,
She sat by the fire and told many a fine tale.

567

Pussy-cat sits by the fire.
 How did she come there?
In walks the little dog,
 Says, "Pussy! are you there?
How do you do, Mistress Pussy?
 Mistress Pussy, how d'ye do?"
"I thank you kindly, little dog,
 I fare as well as you!"

568

A north country version of a very common nursery rhyme, sung by a child, who imitates the crowing of a cock.

Cock-a-doodle-do,
My dad's gane to ploo;
Mammy's lost her pudding-poke,
And knows not what to do.

569

Higglepy Piggleby,
My black hen,
She lays eggs
For gentlemen;
Sometimes nine,
And sometimes ten,
Higglepy Piggleby,
My black hen.

570

Pretty John Watts,
We are troubled with rats,
Will you drive them out of the house?
We have mice, too, in plenty
That feast in the pantry;
But let them stay,
And nibble away;
What harm in a little brown mouse?

571

Jack Sprat
Had a cat,
It had but one ear;
It went to buy butter,
When butter was dear.

572

On Christmas eve I turn'd the spit,
I burnt my fingers, I feel it yet;
The cock-sparrow flew over the table;
The pot began to play with the ladle.

573

See, saw, Margery Daw,
The old hen flew over the malt-house;
She counted her chickens one by one,
Still she missed the little white one,
And this is it, this is it, this is it.

574

Hurly, burly, trumpet trace,
The cow was in the market place,
Some goes far, and some goes near,
But where shall this poor henchman steer?

575

There was an old woman had three cows,
    Rosy, and Colin, and Dun;
Rosy and Colin were sold at the fair,
And Dun broke his head in a fit of despair;
And there was an end of her three cows,
    Rosy, and Colin, and Dun.

576

I'll away yhame,
And tell my dame,
That all my geese
Are gane but yane;

And it's a steg (*gander*),
And it's lost a leg;
And it'll be gane
By I get yhame.

577

Imitated from a pigeon.

Curr dhoo, curr dhoo,
Love me, and I'll love you!

578

I like little pussy, her coat is so warm,
And if I don't hurt her she'll do me no harm;
So I'll not pull her tail, nor drive her away,
But pussy and I very gently will play.

579

Little cock-robin peep'd out of his cabin,
To see the cold winter come in,
Tit for tat, what matter for that,
He'll hide his head under his wing!

580

The pettitoes are little feet,
And the little feet not big;
Great feet belong to the grunting hog,
And the pettitoes to the little pig.

581

Charley Warley had a cow,
Black and white about the brow;
Open the gate and let her go through,
Charley Warley's old cow!

582

I had a little cow;
　Hey-diddle, ho-diddle!
I had a little cow, and it had a little calf;
Hey-diddle, ho-diddle; and there's my song half.

I had a little cow;
　Hey-diddle, ho-diddle!
I had a little cow, and I drove it to the stall;
Hey-diddle, ho-diddle; and there's my song all!

583

The Cock. Lock the dairy door,
　　　　　Lock the dairy door!
The Hen. Chickle, chackle, chee,
　　　　　I haven't got the key!

584

I had a little pony,
　His name was Dapple Grey,
I sent him to a lady,
　To ride a mile away;
She whipped him, she slashed him,
　She rode him through the mire;
I would not lend my pony now
　For all the lady's hire.

585

Bah, bah, black sheep,
　Have you any wool?
Yes, marry, have I,
　Three bags full:

One for my master,
  And one for my dame,
But none for the little boy
  Who cries in the lane.

586

Hussy, hussy, where's your horse?
Hussy, hussy, gone to grass!
Hussy, hussy, fetch him home.
Hussy, hussy, let him alone!

587

Leg over leg,
  As the dog went to Dover;
    When he came to a stile,
  Jump he went over.

588

Rowsty dowt, my fire's all out,
My little dame is not at home!
I'll saddle my cock, and bridle my hen,
And fetch my little dame home again!
Home she came, tritty trot;
She asked for the porridge she left in the pot;
Some she ate and some she shod,
And some she gave to the truckler's dog;
She took up the ladle and knocked its head,
And now poor Dapsy dog is dead.

589

Little boy blue, come blow up your horn,
The sheep's in the meadow, the cow's in the corn;

Where's the little boy that looks after the sheep?
He's under the hay-cock fast asleep.
Will you wake him? No, not I;
For if I do, he'll be sure to cry.

590

Goosey, goosey, gander,
  Where shall I wander?
Up stairs, down stairs,
  And in my lady's chamber:
There I met an old man
  That would not say his prayers;
I took him by the left leg,
  And threw him down stairs.

591

Goosey, goosey, gander,
Who stands yonder?
Little Betsy Baker;
Take her up, and shake her.

Accumulative Stories

592

I sell you the key of the king's garden:
I sell you the string that ties the key, &c.
I sell you the rat that gnawed the string, &c.
I sell you the cat that caught the rat, &c.
I sell you the dog that bit the cat, &c.

593

Traditional pieces are frequently so ancient, that possibility
will not be outraged by conjecturing the John Ball of the
following piece to be the priest who took so distinguished a
part in the rebellion temp. Richard II.

John Ball shot them all;
John Scott made the shot,
  But John Ball shot them all.

John Wyming made the priming,
And John Brammer made the rammer,
And John Scott made the shot,
  But John Ball shot them all.

John Block made the stock,
And John Brammer made the rammer,
And John Wyming made the priming,
And John Scott made the shot,
 But John Ball shot them all.

John Crowder made the powder,
And John Block made the stock,
And John Wyming made the priming,
And John Brammer made the rammer,
And John Scott made the shot,
 But John Ball shot them all.

John Puzzle made the muzzle,
And John Crowder made the powder,
And John Block made the stock,
And John Wyming made the priming,
And John Brammer made the rammer,
And John Scott made the shot,
 But John Ball shot them all.

John Clint made the flint,
And John Puzzle made the muzzle,
And John Crowder made the powder,
And John Block made the stock,
And John Wyming made the priming,
And John Brammer made the rammer,
And John Scott made the shot,
 But John Ball shot them all.

John Patch made the match,
John Clint made the flint,
John Puzzle made the muzzle,
John Crowder made the powder,
John Block made the stock,
John Wyming made the priming,
John Brammer made the rammer,
John Scott made the shot,
 But John Ball shot them all.

594

1. This is the house that Jack built.

2. This is the malt
   That lay in the house that Jack built.

3. This is the rat,
   That ate the malt
   That lay in the house that Jack built.

4. This is the cat,
   That kill'd the rat,
   That ate the malt
   That lay in the house that Jack built.

5. This is the dog,
   That worried the cat,
   That kill'd the rat,
   That ate the malt
   That lay in the house that Jack built.

6. This is the cow with the crumpled horn,
   That toss'd the dog,
   That worried the cat,
   That kill'd the rat,
   That ate the malt
   That lay in the house that Jack built.

7. This is the maiden all forlorn,
   That milk'd the cow with the crumpled horn,
   That tossed the dog,
   That worried the cat,
   That kill'd the rat,
   That ate the malt
   That lay in the house that Jack built.

8. This is the man all tatter'd and torn,
   That kissed the maiden all forlorn,

That milk'd the cow with the crumpled horn,
That tossed the dog,
That worried the cat,
That kill'd the rat,
That ate the malt
That lay in the house that Jack built.

9. This is the priest all shaven and shorn,
That married the man all tatter'd and torn,
That kissed the maiden all forlorn,
That milk'd the cow with the crumpled horn,
That tossed the dog,
That worried the cat,
That kill'd the rat,
That ate the malt,
That lay in the house that Jack built.

10. This is the cock that crow'd in the morn,
That waked the priest all shaven and shorn,
That married the man all tatter'd and torn,
That kissed the maiden all forlorn,
That milk'd the cow with the crumpled horn,
That tossed the dog,
That worried the cat,
That kill'd the rat,
That ate the malt
That lay in the house that Jack built.

11. This is the farmer sowing his corn,
That kept the cock that crow'd in the morn,
That waked the priest all shaven and shorn,
That married the man all tatter'd and torn,
That kissed the maiden all forlorn,
That milk'd the cow with the crumpled horn,
That tossed the dog,
That worried the cat,
That kill'd the rat,
That ate the malt
That lay in the house that Jack built.

595

The original of "The house that Jack built" is presumed to be a hymn in *Sepher Haggadah*, fol. 23, a translation of which is here given. The historical interpretation was first given by P. N. Leberecht, at Leipsic, in 1731, and is printed in the "Christian Reformer", vol. xvii. p. 28. The original is in the Chaldee language, and it may be mentioned that a very fine Hebrew manuscript of the fable, with illuminations, is in the possession of George Offer, Esq. of Hackney.

1. *A kid, a kid*, my father bought
   For two pieces of money: A kid, a kid.

2. Then came *the cat*, and ate the kid,
   That my father bought
   For two pieces of money: A kid, a kid.

3. Then came *the dog*, and bit the cat,
   That ate the kid,
   That my father bought
   For two pieces of money: A kid, a kid.

4. Then came *the staff*, and beat the dog,
   That bit the cat,
   That ate the kid,
   That my father bought
   For two pieces of money: A kid, a kid.

5. Then came *the fire*, and burned the staff,
   That beat the dog,
   That bit the cat,
   That ate the kid,
   That my father bought
   For two pieces of money: A kid, a kid.

6. Then came *the water*, and quenched the fire,
   That burned the staff,
   That beat the dog,
   That bit the cat,
   That ate the kid,
   That my father bought
   For two pieces of money: A kid, a kid.

7. Then came *the ox*, and drank the water,
That quenched the fire,
That burned the staff,
That beat the dog,
That bit the cat,
That ate the kid,
That my father bought
For two pieces of money: A kid, a kid.

8. Then came *the butcher*, and slew the ox,
That drank the water,
That quenched the fire,
That burned the staff,
That beat the dog,
That bit the cat,
That ate the kid,
That my father bought
For two pieces of money: A kid, a kid.

9. Then came *the angel of death*, and killed the butcher,
That slew the ox,
That drank the water,
That quenched the fire,
That burned the staff,
That beat the dog,
That bit the cat,
That ate the kid,
That my father bought
For two pieces of money: A kid, a kid.

10. Then came *the Holy One*, blessed be He!
And killed the angel of death,
That killed the butcher,
That slew the ox,
That drank the water,
That quenched the fire,
That burned the staff,
That beat the dog,
That bit the cat,

That ate the kid,
That my father bought
For two pieces of money: A kid, a kid.

The following is the interpetation:

1. The kid, which was one of the pure animals, denotes the Hebrews.

The father, by whom it was purchased, is Jehovah, who represents himself as sustaining this relation to the Hebrew nation. The two pieces of money signify Moses and Aaron, through whose mediation the Hebrews were brought out of Egypt.

2. The cat denotes the Assyrians, by whom the ten tribes were carried into captivity.

3. The dog is symbolical of the Babylonians.

4. The staff signifies the Persians.

5. The fire indicates the Grecian empire under Alexander the Great.

6. The water betokens the Roman, or the fourth of the great monarchies to whose dominions the Jews were subjected.

7. The ox is a symbol of the Saracens, who subdued Palestine, and brought it under the caliphate.

8. The butcher that killed the ox denotes the crusaders, by whom the Holy Land was wrested out of the hands of the Saracens.

9. The angel of death signifies the Turkish power, by which the land of Palestine was taken from the Franks, and to which it is still subject.

10. The commencement of the tenth stanza is designed to show that God will take signal vengeance on the Turks, immediately after whose overthrow the Jews are to be restored to their own land, and live under the government of their long-expected Messiah.

596

"An old woman was sweeping her house, and she found a little crooked sixpence. 'What,' said she, 'shall I do with this little sixpence? I will go to market, and buy a little pig.' As she was coming home, she came to a stile: the piggy would not go over the stile.

"She went a little further, and she met a dog. So she said to the dog, 'Dog! bite pig; piggy won't go over the stile; and I shan't get home to-night.' But the dog would not.

"She went a little further, and she met a stick. So she said, 'Stick! stick! beat dog; dog won't bite pig; piggy won't get over the stile; and I shan't get home to-night.' But the stick would not.

"She went a little further, and she met a fire. So she said, 'Fire! fire! burn stick; stick won't beat dog; dog won't bite pig,' (*and so forth, always repeating the foregoing words*). But the fire would not.

"She went a little further, and she met some water. So she said, 'Water! water! quench fire; fire won't burn stick.' &c. But the water would not.

"She went a little further, and she met an ox. So she said, 'Ox! ox! drink water; water won't quench fire,' &c. But the ox would not.

"She went a little further, and she met a butcher. So she said, 'Butcher! butcher! kill ox; ox won't drink water,' &c. But the butcher would not.

"She went a little further, and she met a rope. So she said, 'Rope! rope! hang butcher; butcher won't kill ox,' &c. But the rope would not.

"She went a little further, and she met a rat. So she said, 'Rat! rat! gnaw rope: rope won't hang butcher,' &c. But the rat would not.

"She went a little further, and she met a cat. So she said, 'Cat! cat! kill rat; rat won't gnaw rope,' &c. But the cat said to her, 'If you will go to yonder cow, and fetch me a saucer of milk, I will kill the rat.' So away went the old woman to the cow.

"But the cow said to her, 'If you will go to yonder haystack,* and fetch me a handful of hay, I'll give you the milk.' So away went the old woman to the haystack; and she brought the hay to the cow.

"As soon as the cow had eaten the hay, she gave the old woman the milk; and away she went with it in a saucer to the cat.

"As soon as the cat had lapped up the milk, the cat began to kill the rat; the rat began to gnaw the rope; the rope began to hang the butcher; the butcher began to kill the ox; the ox began to drink the water; the water began to quench the fire; the fire began to burn the stick; the stick began to beat the dog; the dog began to bite the pig; the little pig in a fright jumped over the stile; and so the old woman got home that night."

---

* Or haymakers, proceeding thus in the stead of the rest of this paragraph: "And fetch me a wisp of hay, I'll give you the milk.—So away the old woman went, but the haymakers said to her,—'If you will go to yonder stream, and fetch us a bucket of water, we'll give you the hay'. So away the old woman went, but when she got to the stream, she found the bucket was full of holes. So she covered the bottom with pebbles, and then she filled the bucket with water, and away she went back with it to the hay-makers; and they gave her a wisp of hay."

597

Titty Mouse and Tatty Mouse both lived in a house,
Titty Mouse went a leasing, and Tatty Mouse went a leasing,
  So they both went a leasing.

Titty Mouse leased an ear of corn, and Tatty Mouse leased an ear of
    corn,
  So they both leased an ear of corn.

Titty Mouse made a pudding, and Tatty Mouse made a pudding,
  So they both made a pudding.

And Tatty Mouse put her pudding into the pot to boil,
  But when Titty went to put hers in, the pot tumbled over, and
    scalded her to death.

Then Tatty sat down and wept; then a three-legged stool said,
Tatty, why do you weep? Titty's dead, said Tatty, and so I weep;
then said the stool, I'll hop, so the stool hopped; then a besom in
the corner of the room said, Stool, why do you hop? Oh! said the
stool, Titty's dead, and Tatty weeps, and so I hop; then said the
besom, I'll sweep, so the besom began to sweep; then said the door,
Besom, why do you sweep? Oh! said the besom, Titty's dead, and
Tatty weeps, and the stool hops, and so I sweep; then said the door,
I'll jar, so the door jarred; then said the window, Door, why do you
jar? Oh! said the door, Titty's dead, and Tatty weeps, and the stool
hops, and the besom sweeps, and so I jar; then said the window, I'll
creak, so the window creaked. Now there was an old form outside
the house, and when the window creaked, the form said, Window,
why do you creak? Oh! said the window, Titty's dead, and Tatty
weeps, and the stool hops, and the besom sweeps, the door jars, and
so I creak; then said the old form, I'll run round the house; then
the old form ran round the house. Now there was a fine large
walnut-tree growing by the cottage, and the tree said to the form,
Form, why do you run round the house? Oh! said the form,
Titty's dead, and Tatty weeps, and the stool hops, and the besom
sweeps, the door jars, and the window creaks, and so I run round
the house; then said the walnut-tree, I'll shed my leaves, so the

walnut tree shed all its beautiful green leaves. Now there was a little bird perched on one of the boughs of the tree, and when all the leaves fell, it said, Walnut-tree, why do you shed your leaves? Oh! said the tree, Titty's dead, and Tatty weeps, the stool hops, and the besom sweeps, the door jars, and the window creaks, the old form runs round the house, and so I shed my leaves; then said the little bird, I'll moult all my feathers, so he moulted all his pretty feathers. Now there was a little girl walking below, carrying a jug of milk for her brothers' and sisters' supper, and when she saw the poor little bird moult all its feathers, she said, Little bird, why do you moult all your feathers? Oh! said the little bird, Titty's dead, and Tatty weeps, the stool hops, and the besom sweeps, the door jars, and the window creaks, the old form runs round the house, the walnut-tree sheds its leaves, and so I moult all my feathers; then said the little girl, I'll spill the milk, so she dropt the pitcher and spilt the milk. Now there was an old man just by on the top of a ladder thatching a rick, and when he saw the little girl spill the milk, he said, Little girl, what do you mean by spilling the milk, your little brothers and sisters must go without their supper; then said the little girl, Titty's dead, and Tatty weeps, the stool hops, and the besom sweeps, the door jars, and the window creaks, the old form runs round the house, the walnut-tree sheds all its leaves, the little bird moults all its feathers, and so I spill the milk; Oh! said the old man, then I'll tumble off the ladder and break my neck; and when the old man broke his neck, the great walnut-tree fell down with a crash, and upset the old form and house, and the house falling knocked the window out, and the window knocked the door down, and the door upset the besom, the besom upset the stool, and poor little Tatty Mouse was buried beneath the ruins.

Local

598

There was a little nobby colt,
His name was Nobby Gray;
His head was made of pouce straw;
   His tail was made of hay;
      He could ramble, he could trot,
      He could carry a mustard-pot,
      Round the town of Woodstock,
Hey, Jenny, hey!

599

King's Sutton is a pretty town,
   And lies all in a valley:
There is a pretty ring of bells,
   Besides a bowling-alley:
Wine and liquor in good store,
   Pretty maidens plenty:
Can a man desire more?
   There ain't such a town in twenty.

600

The little priest of Felton,
The little priest of Felton,
He kill'd a mouse within his house,
And ne'er a one to help him.

601

The following verses are said by Aubrey to have been sung in
his time by the girls of Oxfordshire in a sport called *Leap
Candle*, which is now obsolete. See Thoms's "Anecdotes and
Traditions", p. 96.

The tailor of Bicester,
   He has but one eye;
He cannot cut a pair of green galagaskins,
   If he were to try.

602

Dick and Tom, Will and John,
Brought me from Nottingham.

603

At Brill on the Hill,
The wind blows shrill,
The cook no meat can dress;
At Stow in the Wold
The wind blows cold,—
I know no more than this.

604

A man went a hunting at Reigate,
And wished to leap over a high gate;
Says the owner, "Go round,
With your gun and your hound,
For you never shall leap over my gate."

605

Driddlety drum, driddlety drum,
There you see the beggars are come;
Some are here, and some are there,
And some are gone to Chidley fair.

606

Little boy, pretty boy, where was you born?
In Lincolnshire, master: come blow the cow's horn.
A halfpenny pudding, a penny pie,
A shoulder of mutton, and that love I.

607

My father and mother,
My uncle and aunt,
Be all gone to Norton,
But Little Jack and I.
A little bit of powdered beef,
And a great net of cabbage,
The best meal I have had to-day
Is a good bowl of porridge.

608

I lost my mare in Lincoln lane,
And couldn't tell where to find her,
Till she came home both lame and blind,
With never a tail behind her.

609

Cripple Dick upon a stick,
And Sandy on a sow,
Riding away to Galloway,
To buy a pound o' woo.

610

Little lad, little lad, where wast thou born?
Far off in Lancashire, under a thorn,
Where they sup sour milk in a ram's horn.

EIGHTEENTH CLASS

Relics

611

The girl in the lane, that couldn't speak plain,
Cried: "Gobble, gobble, gobble:"
The man on the hill, that couldn't stand still,
Went hobble, hobble, hobble.

612

Hinx, minx! the old witch winks,
The fat begins to fry:
There's nobody at home but jumping Joan,
Father, mother, and I.

613

Baby and I
Were baked in a pie,
The gravy was wonderful hot:
We had nothing to pay
To the baker that day,
And so we crept out of the pot.

614

What are little boys made of, made of,
What are little boys made of?
Snaps and snails, and puppy-dog's tails;
And that's what little boys are made of, made of.

What are little girls made of, made of,
What are little girls made of?
Sugar and spice, and all that's nice;
And that's what little girls are made of, made of.

615

If a body meet a body,
In a field of fitches;
Can a body tell a body
Where a body itches?

616

Charley wag,
Ate the pudding and left the bag.

617

Girls and boys, come out to play,
The moon doth shine as bright as day;
Leave your supper, and leave your sleep,
And come with your playfellows into the street.
Come with a whoop, come with a call,
Come with a good will or not at all.
Up the ladder and down the wall,
A halfpenny roll will serve us all.
You find milk, and I'll find flour,
And we'll have a pudding in half an hour.

618

Hannah Bantry in the pantry,
    Eating a mutton-bone;
How she gnawed it, how she clawed it,
    When she found she was alone!

619

Rain, rain, go away,
Come again another day,
Little Arthur wants to play.

620

Little girl, little girl, where have you been?
Gathering roses to give to the queen.
Little girl, little girl, what gave she you?
She gave me a diamond as big as my shoe.

621

Hark, hark,
The dogs do bark,
Beggars are coming to town;
Some in jags,
Some in rags,
And some in velvet gown.

622

We're all in the dumps,
    For diamonds are trumps;
The kittens are gone to St Paul's!
    The babies are bit,
    The moon's in a fit,
And the houses are built without walls.

623

What's the news of the day,
Good neighbour, I pray?
They say the balloon
Is gone up to the moon.

624

Little Mary Ester,
Sat upon a tester,
Eating of curds and whey;
There came a little spider,
And sat him down beside her,
And frightened Mary Ester away.

625

Shake a leg, wag a leg, when will you gang?
At midsummer, mother, when the days are lang.

626

Willy boy, Willy boy, where are you going?
I'll go with you if I may.
I'm going to the meadow to see them a mowing,
I'm going to help them make hay.

627

To market, to market, a gallop, a trot,
To buy some meat to put in the pot;
Threepence a quarter, a groat a side,
If it hadn't been kill'd, it must have died.

628

Come, let's to bed,
Says Sleepy-head;
Tarry a while, says Slow:
Put on the pot,
Says Greedy-gut,
Let's sup before we go.

629

How many days has my baby to play?
Saturday, Sunday, Monday,
Tuesday, Wednesday, Thursday, Friday,
Saturday, Sunday, Monday.

630

Daffy-down-dilly has come up to town,
In a yellow petticoat, and a green gown.

631

Little Tom Tucker
Sings for his supper;
What shall he eat?
White bread and butter.
How shall he cut it
Without e'er a knife?
How will he be married
Without e'er a wife?

632

I can weave diaper thick, thick, thick,
And I can weave diaper thin,
I can weave diaper out of doors
And I can weave diaper in.

633

The following is quoted in the song of Mad Tom. See my Introduction to Shakespeare's "Mids. Night's Dream", p. 55.

The man in the moon drinks claret,
But he is a dull Jack-a-Dandy;
Would he know a sheep's head from a carrot,
He should learn to drink cider and brandy.

634

A marching air.

Darby and Joan were dress'd in black,
Sword and buckle behind their back;
Foot for foot, and knee for knee,
Turn about Darby's company.

635

Barber, barber, shave a pig,
How many hairs will make a wig?
"Four and twenty, that's enough."
Give the barber a pinch of snuff.

636

If all the seas were one sea,
What a *great* sea that would be!
And if all the trees were one tree,
What a *great* tree that would be!
And if all the axes were one axe,
What a *great* axe that would be!
And if all the men were one man,
What a *great* man he would be!
And if the *great* man took the *great* axe,
And cut down the *great* tree,
And let it fall into the *great* sea,
What a splish splash *that* would be!

637

I had a little moppet,
I put it in my pocket,
And fed it with corn and hay;
Then came a proud beggar,
And swore he would have her,
And stole little moppet away.

638

The barber shaved the mason,
As I suppose
Cut off his nose,
And popp'd it in a bason.

639

Little Tommy Tacket,
Sits upon his cracket;
Half a yard of cloth will make him coat and jacket;
Make him coat and jacket,
Trousers to the knee.
And if you will not have him, you may let him be.

640

Peg, peg, with a wooden leg,
Her father was a miller:
He tossed the dumpling at her head,
And said he could not kill her.

641

Parson Darby wore a black gown,
And every button cost half-a-crown;
From port to port, and toe to toe,
Turn the ship and away we go!

642

When Jacky's a very good boy,
  He shall have cakes and a custard;
But when he does nothing but cry,
  He shall have nothing but mustard.

643

Blow, wind, blow! and go, mill, go!
That the miller may grind his corn;
  That the baker may take it,
  And into rolls make it,
And send us some hot in the morn.

644

The Quaker's wife got up to bake,
  Her children all about her,
She gave them every one a cake,
  And the miller wants his moulter.

645

Wash, hands, wash,
  Daddy's gone to plough;
If you want your hands wash'd,
  Have them wash'd now.

A formula for making young children submit to the operation
of having their hands washed. *Mutatis mutandis*, the lines will
serve as a specific for everything of the kind, as brushing hair,
&c.

646

My little old man and I fell out,
I'll tell you what 'twas all about:
I had money, and he had none,
And that's the way the row begun.

647

Who comes here?
 A grenadier.
What do you want?
 A pot of beer.
Where is your money?
 I've forgot.
Get you gone,
 You drunken sot!

648

Go to bed, Tom!
Go to bed, Tom!
Drunk or sober,
Go to bed, Tom!

649

As I went over the water,
 The water went over me,
I heard an old woman crying,
 Will you buy some furmity?

650

High diddle doubt, my candle's out,
 My little maid is not at home:
Saddle my hog, and bridle my dog,
 And fetch my little maid home.

651

Around the green gravel the grass grows green,
And all the pretty maids are plain to be seen;
Wash them with milk, and clothe them with silk,
And write their names with a pen and ink.

652

As I was going to sell my eggs,
I met a man with bandy legs,
Bandy legs and crooked toes,
I tripped up his heels, and he fell on his nose.

653

Old Sir Simon the king,
And young Sir Simon the 'squire,
And old Mrs Hickabout
Kicked Mrs Kickabout
Round about our coal fire!

654

A good child, a good child,
As I suppose you be,
Never laughed nor smiled
At the tickling of your knee.

655

Jacky, come give me thy fiddle
If ever thou mean to thrive;
Nay, I'll not give my fiddle,
To any man alive.

If I should give my fiddle,
They'll think that I'm gone mad,
For many a joyful day
My fiddle and I have had.

656

Blenky my nutty-cock,
Blenk him away;

My nutty-cock's never
  Been blenk'd to-day.
What wi' carding and spinning on't wheel:
We've never had time to blenk nutty-cock weel;
But let to-morrow come ever so sune,
My nutty-cock it sall be blenk'd by nune.

657

To market, to market, to buy a plum-cake,
Back again, back again, baby is late;
To market, to market, to buy a plum-bun,
Back again, back again, market is done.

658

St Thomas's-day is past and gone,
And Christmas is a-most a-come,
    Maidens arise,
    And make your pies,
And save poor tailor Bobby some.

659

How do you do, neighbour?
Neighbour, how do you do?
  I am pretty well,
And how does Cousin Sue do?
  She's pretty well,
And sends her duty to you,
  So does bonnie Nell.
Good lack, how does she do?

Index of First Lines